VOLUME EDITORS

JESSICA WOLFENDALE is Assistant Professor of Philosophy at West Virginia University, and perhaps a little too fond of vintage clothing. She is the author of *Torture and the Military Profession* (2007) and has published extensively on the ethics of torture, military ethics, and applied ethics.

JEANETTE KENNETT is Professor of Moral Psychology at Macquarie University, Sydney, Australia. She is the author of *Agency and Responsibility* (2001) and has published widely on topics including empathy, addiction, self-control, advertising, and love and friendship.

D1279865

SERIES EDITOR

FRITZ ALLHOFF is an Assistant Professor in the Philosophy Department at Western Michigan University, as well as a Senior Research Fellow at the Australian National University's Centre for Applied Philosophy and Public Ethics. In addition to editing the *Philosophy for Everyone* series, Allhoff is the volume editor or co-editor for several titles, including *Wine & Philosophy* (Wiley-Blackwell, 2007), *Whiskey & Philosophy* (with Marcus P. Adams, Wiley, 2009), and *Food & Philosophy* (with Dave Monroe, Wiley-Blackwell, 2007). His academic research interests engage various facets of applied ethics, ethical theory, and the history and philosophy of science.

PHILOSOPHY FOR EVERYONE

Series editor: Fritz Allhoff

Not so much a subject matter, philosophy is a way of thinking. Thinking not just about the Big Questions, but about little ones too. This series invites everyone to ponder things they care about, big or small, significant, serious … or just curious.

Running & Philosophy:
A Marathon for the Mind
Edited by Michael W. Austin

Wine & Philosophy:
A Symposium on Thinking and Drinking
Edited by Fritz Allhoff

Food & Philosophy:
Eat, Think and Be Merry
Edited by Fritz Allhoff and Dave Monroe

Beer & Philosophy:
The Unexamined Beer Isn't Worth Drinking
Edited by Steven D. Hales

Whiskey & Philosophy:
A Small Batch of Spirited Ideas
Edited by Fritz Allhoff
and Marcus P. Adams

College Sex – Philosophy for Everyone: Philosophers With Benefits
Edited by Michael Bruce
and Robert M. Stewart

Cycling – Philosophy for Everyone:
A Philosophical Tour de Force
Edited by Jesús Ilundáin-Agurruza
and Michael W. Austin

Climbing – Philosophy for Everyone:
Because It's There
Edited by Stephen E. Schmid

Hunting – Philosophy for Everyone:
In Search of the Wild Life
Edited by Nathan Kowalsky

Christmas – Philosophy for Everyone:
Better Than a Lump of Coal
Edited by Scott C. Lowe

Cannabis – Philosophy for Everyone:
What Were We Just Talking About?
Edited by Dale Jacquette

Porn – Philosophy for Everyone:
How to Think With Kink
Edited by Dave Monroe

Serial Killers – Philosophy for Everyone: Being and Killing
Edited by S. Waller

Dating – Philosophy for Everyone:
Flirting With Big Ideas
Edited by Kristie Miller and Marlene Clark

Gardening – Philosophy for Everyone:
Cultivating Wisdom
Edited by Dan O'Brien

Motherhood – Philosophy for Everyone:
The Birth of Wisdom
Edited by Sheila Lintott

Fatherhood – Philosophy for Everyone:
The Dao of Daddy
Edited by Lon S. Nease
and Michael W. Austin

Fashion – Philosophy for Everyone:
Thinking with Style
Edited by Jessica Wolfendale
and Jeanette Kennett

Yoga – Philosophy for Everyone:
Bending Mind and Body
Edited by Liz Stillwaggon Swan

Forthcoming books in the series:

Blues – Philosophy for Everyone:
Thinking Deep About Feeling Low
Edited by Abrol Fairweather and Jesse Steinberg

Sailing – Philosophy for Everyone:
A Place of Perpetual Undulation
Edited by Patrick Goold

Tattoos – Philosophy for Everyone:
I Ink, Therefore I Am
Edited by Rob Arp

Edited by Jessica Wolfendale and Jeanette Kennett

FASHION

PHILOSOPHY FOR EVERYONE

Thinking with Style

Foreword by Jennifer Baumgardner

A John Wiley & Sons, Ltd., Publication

This edition first published 2011
© 2011 Blackwell Publishing Ltd.

Blackwell Publishing was acquired by John Wiley & Sons in February 2007. Blackwell's publishing program has been merged with Wiley's global Scientific, Technical, and Medical business to form Wiley-Blackwell.

Registered Office
John Wiley & Sons Ltd, The Atrium, Southern Gate, Chichester, West Sussex, PO19 8SQ, UK

Editorial Offices
350 Main Street, Malden, MA 02148-5020, USA
9600 Garsington Road, Oxford, OX4 2DQ, UK
The Atrium, Southern Gate, Chichester, West Sussex, PO19 8SQ, UK

For details of our global editorial offices, for customer services, and for information about how to apply for permission to reuse the copyright material in this book please see our website at www.wiley.com/wiley-blackwell.

The right of Jessica Wolfendale and Jeanette Kennett to be identified as the authors of the editorial material in this work has been asserted in accordance with the UK Copyright, Designs and Patents Act 1988.

Library of Congress Cataloging-in-Publication Data

Fashion – philosophy for everyone: thinking with style / edited by Jessica Wolfendale and Jeanette Kennett.
    p.   cm. – (Philosophy for everyone; 40)
  Includes bibliographical references and index.
  ISBN 978-1-4051-9990-2 (pbk.)
1. Fashion–Philosophy.   2. Clothing and dress–Philosophy.   I. Kennett, Jeanette.
II. Wolfendale, Jessica, 1973–
  GT521.F38 2011
  391.001–dc22

                                        2011015488

A catalogue record for this book is available from the British Library.

This book is published in the following electronic formats: ePDFs 9781444345520; Wiley Online Library 9781444345568; ePub 9781444345544; Mobi 9781444345551

Set in 10/12.5pt Plantin by SPi Publisher Services, Pondicherry, India
Printed in Malaysia by Ho Printing (M) Sdn Bhd

1   2011

I'd like to dedicate this book to my mother for letting me wear whatever I wanted when I was growing up, no matter how outrageous; to my late grandmother for her amazing dress-up box that included a fabulously chic leopard print hat, and to my sister for her sometimes too honest but always helpful critiques of my outfits!

– Jessica Wolfendale

I dedicate this book to the 1960s and the people in it who shaped my interest in fashion: my mother whose wardrobe was a treasure trove of hats for a small girl to try on when she was out, my father whose collection of early 1960s shirts and shoes would make a vintage shopper weep for joy, and my then teenage sisters, whose dresses, make up and hairstyles are indelibly imprinted on my memory.

– Jeanette Kennett

CONTENTS

FOREWORD

For the past couple of years, I have nursed a persistent sense that I'm not trying hard enough. No one is saying this to me; I simply feel it instinctively. The source of this inadequacy, you ask? While I could definitely point to my writing (*Does this read as if I'm a fifth grader?*) or my parenting (*Always attempting to avoid tedious nurturing!*) or my finances (*Sacre Bleu!*), the realm in which I'm slacking is fashion. As I step into my navy blue, heavily scuffed Sven clogs each day, perhaps matched with jeans and a t-shirt and cardigan or complementing a shapeless summer sundress, I wonder: am I *too* comfortable? Cutting too many corners regarding my public armor?

My chronic clog wearing feels akin to eating Honeynut Cheerios for dinner every night – a far cry from psychic annihilation, but not really living a full life, either. Socrates might see my lack of style as a good thing. As quoted in "Slaves to Fashion," one essay in the surprising, provocative collection you hold in your hands, Socrates says that "the genuine philosopher disdains"[1] fashion and, in doing so, the authors of that essay conclude, "he practices dying."[2]

Disdain of worldliness works for Socrates, but my philosophy, feminism, is devoted to what it means to live. Feminism is deeply entwined with creating life – both procreation and self-creation. Sartorially, my issue is this: I, a feminist writer of 40 and mother of two, do not want to *dress* "like a feminist" (or a mother, for that matter. Mom jeans. *Blecch*). In short, I don't want to be reduced to the clichés or stereotypes of the identity that has liberated me. One of my closest colleagues calls it the fear of "becoming a purple[3] feminist" – purple sneakers, purple over-sized

"This is what a feminist looks like" t-shirts, "ethnic" (though not your own ethnicity) tops, big jewelry, and "natural" hair. Perhaps a hemp pantsuit in Grimace grape for a special meeting?

Let's contrast that look with fashionable dress: heels, lustrous or chicly shorn hair, clothing made to flatter and shape rather than obscure the body, and accessories that charm or are beautiful objects. Nearly 160 years ago, first wave feminists called for dress reform, creating a harem pants ensemble that was practical and comfortable, and shockingly controversial because it enabled movement and freedom). Then, 40 or so years ago, feminists critiqued the beauty standards applied to women (These critiques contained at least the following elements: first, women's fashions are designed to not just symbolize but maintain women's weakness via straight skirts (*only small steps, please Ma'am*), shoes that prohibit running, and necklines cut in a way that require poise to keep in place. Second, fashion colludes to reduce women to objects, rather than enabling their full humanity. And third, the constant change of fashions aimed at women means that we bankrupt our finances and energy keeping up with this trivial pursuit.

I have grown up with these critiques alongside enduring beauty standards and fashion ideals. Having access to both critique and commodity means that my view of fashion might be different in 2011 than a sister feminist's view in 1970. To wit, the high heel can be seen as, like the corset, a symbol of women's oppression, but I actually feel equally oppressed by my clogs – tamped down by my own cowardice to break out of them. Recently, at a birthday party for a friend, I donned a silk georgette jewel-toned swing dress and, in a crisis of confidence, opted to wear blue ballet flats rather than my sparkly pewter heels. The minute I got to the event, I regretted my decision. All of the women looked amazing, and they all wore heels. It was as if I had left the house with my hair in rollers. And I wore the flats not because I thought they looked better or even out of a real commitment to anti-fashion *à la* Andrea Dworkin, but because standing that tall in the world required grace and confidence I wasn't sure I could muster (but I could have, and I should have).

Fashion can constrain, and certainly those constraints mirror other ways that women are hobbled (or asked to self-fetter), but a beautifully shod pair of feet is also an example of finesse and effort. When you wear sweatpants, you say, "I don't have a body, I'm basically shapeless underneath this stretchy shroud." But you do you have a body under there, and feminism is devoted to respecting one's body. Feminism also encourages women to push beyond comfort, recognizing the link between risk and accomplishment. A woman might be more comfortable living under patriarchy, for example: not paying bills, barred from serious endeavor. But effort and achievement is so much sweeter than mere ease.

So, can you be a serious person and be … fashionable? The answer has to be yes. At the end of the day, it's just as oppressive to be told you can't wear Miucci Prada as it is to be told you must. To return to my initial conceit – my creeping sense of laziness and inadequacy – the malaise is deeply connected to how I'm currently dressed (taupe hoodie, white jeans, and blue clogs, for the record). How each of us handles the barrier between public and pubic conveys much about our own values and self-image. I believe that being "above" fashion can be a principled stance, or it can be a mask for someone who is afraid to harness the power of self-presentation. For me, sliding into generic and unconscious comfort is dying a little, but not in that good way that Socrates liked.

I strongly self-identify with a marginalized and stereotyped political philosophy *and* I desire not to be trapped by the narrow images associated with my calling. Fashion aids and abets my self-creation. (I have evidence that having flair invites younger people into feminism, too. Courtney Martin, a writer 10 years my junior, has written that her feminist click was seeing me speak at her school wearing fishnet stockings and realizing that she could manifest a personal style and still be a feminist.)[4] Some feminists critique fashion as accessing a privilege by buying clothing, which requires money, and cashing in on the unequally distributed advantage of beauty. But it has always rankled me that it's only feminists whom we require to be so pure and opt out of pastimes like shopping.

Samantha Brennan writes in this book, "not worrying about fashion, or claiming to, is itself a sign of privilege."[5] So true. As an older single feminist friend of mine has remarked, the older she gets, the more carefully she has to dress so that she doesn't look like a bag lady. It's a privilege of the young, the thin, the married, and the clearly WASPy to not have to dress with an eye toward ameliorating people's negative assumptions.

Even as I consider the conditions under which clothing is made, deplore racist-sexist-homophobic-ableist beauty standards and resist a capitalism that encourages me to buy things I don't need, getting myself dressed is a big part of life. Sometimes a clog is just a clog. But sometimes a clog means I'm practicing dying.

– Jennifer Baumgardner, New York City, April 2011

NOTES

1 Plato, *Phaedo*, 64a–67-e.
2 Lauren Ashwell and Rae Langton, "Slaves to Fashion," this volume.
3 Purple being a traditional color of the suffrage movement in England and later in the US.
4 Courtney E. Martin, "Not My Mother's Hose," in *Click: When We Knew We Were Feminists* (Berkeley, CA: Seal Press, 2010), pp. 89–93.
5 Samantha Brennan, "Sexual Identity, Gender Identity and Fashion: Why Recognition Matters," this volume.

ACKNOWLEDGMENTS

For both of us, fashion is important and always has been. One of us began wearing vintage clothes at age 15 (and still misses the fabulous 1960s cocktail dress she wore to her High School prom) and has never stopped; the other has long been fascinated by icons of style, and rates a visit to a Vivienne Westwood or haute couture fashion exhibition well above a gallery of Constables. We both love to browse vintage clothing shops, watch *Project Runway* and experiment with different styles, colors, patterns, textures, and decades. Yet we work in a field in which fashion is largely ignored, if not outright dismissed as vain and trivial, and so at times we have each struggled with the fear that our interest in fashion is incompatible with being serious philosophers. But one afternoon in 2008, over perhaps one too many gin and tonics, we began talking about what fashion means to us, and discovered that far from being a silly or trivial topic, fashion raises many different and important questions. Our own experiences with fashion and shopping led us to think more carefully about how fashion shapes, liberates, and yet sometimes constrains identity, and how fashion can make us feel creative and artistic, yet can at times also seem conformist, limiting, and burdensome. We realized that, far from being a subject rightly ignored by serious philosophers, fashion touches on and has implications for many important areas of philosophy, including ethics, aesthetics, identity, and social and political philosophy.

Inspired by our afternoon of (restrained) drinking and chatting, we decided that it was time for philosophy to take fashion seriously. We wrote to philosophers working in diverse areas of philosophy to ask if they would contribute to a collection on fashion and, somewhat to our surprise, discovered that there were many who agreed with us that fashion *was* important to philosophy – and not only because so many philosophers could use some fashion advice! It turned out that, particularly for women philosophers, the worry that fashion and serious philosophy were incompatible was a common one, and so it was reassuring to see how quickly it became apparent that fashion is something that philosophy *should* pay attention to. We were excited and inspired by the variety of topics suggested by our contributors – and we quickly realized how valuable this book could be both to philosophers and for anyone interested in fashion.

The journey from our afternoon chat in 2008 to the book that you hold in your hands has been fascinating and thought provoking for both of us. We would like to express our deep gratitude to our contributors for the interesting, challenging, and insightful chapters they have written. Their willingness to engage wholeheartedly with exploring the philosophical side of fashion (and responding to our feedback and comments) from many different angles is inspiring, and we are extremely impressed with the quality of the contributions to this book, and with the depth and thought they display.

This book would not have been possible without the support of the *Philosophy for Everyone* series editor Fritz Allhoff, who encouraged us to see the wide appeal of this topic for everyone, not just philosophers. We also wish to thank Jeff Dean and Tiffany Mok from Wiley-Blackwell for their continued interest and encouragement during the book's production and Jennifer Baumgardner for her engaging and reflective foreword. Of course this book would not have been completed without the continuing inspiration we both find in fashion – from browsing fashion blogs to visiting Graceland in Memphis, vintage clothing fairs in Canberra, and fashion runways in Melbourne, to encouraging each other to explore new styles, fashion remains for us a source of creativity and delight, and an exciting and challenging way of bringing together the joy of dressing up with the world of ideas.

Finally, to the readers of this volume – we hope this book shows you new and exciting ways to think about fashion. And remember, in the words of Coco Chanel, "Fashion is not something that exists in dresses only. Fashion is in the sky, in the street, fashion has to do with ideas, the way we live, what is happening."

Jessica Wolfendale,
West Virginia University

Jeanette Kennett
Macquarie University, Sydney

INTRODUCTION

Who Cares about Fashion?

Why should philosophy pay attention to fashion? Not only are many philosophers conspicuous for their lack of personal style and taste (as a quick survey of any gathering of philosophers will confirm) but fashion also seems to be a topic about which philosophy has had little to say. As Marguerite La Caze points out, philosophers have tended to hold fashion in contempt – to view it as a topic unworthy of serious analysis. What we wear and how we adorn ourselves are seen as matters of taste and personal preference – of mere vanity and social conformity. It seems a waste of valuable time to think about fashion. If anything, we should think about fashion less! When there are so many serious issues (the environment, global poverty, war, and so on) that require urgent attention, worrying about what to wear, what's trendy, how much to spend, and where to shop seems like a moral failing. After all, we rarely praise people for being vain! Surely, as the philosopher Peter Singer argues, we should spend our spare money and

Fashion – Philosophy for Everyone: Thinking with Style, First Edition.
Edited by Jessica Wolfendale and Jeanette Kennett.
© 2011 Blackwell Publishing Ltd. Published 2011 by Blackwell Publishing Ltd.

time on programs that aim to alleviate poverty, starvation, and disease in the developing world, rather than wasting it on items that serve no important needs. Can we justify spending time and money on something as ephemeral as fashion?

This attitude toward fashion may be common among philosophers but it is not well founded. As this volume makes clear, fashion raises numerous important and interesting philosophical issues, many of which have not been well recognized or addressed in philosophy. In thinking about fashion we encounter questions in art and aesthetics, ethics, personal and social identity, political visibility and recognition, freedom and oppression, and the intersection between our bodies, our clothes, and science and technology. To dismiss fashion as philosophically uninteresting is therefore to ignore the rich and diverse set of questions raised by our interest in and practices surrounding, dress, adornment, and style. Fashion does *matter*. Fashion matters to people, and fashion should matter to philosophy.

Being Fashionable and Being Cool

Just what is it that makes an item of clothing fashionable? What is the property of being fashionable? We have an intuitive sense of what is and is not fashionable at any given time, but it is remarkably difficult to explain *how* we know this, and what it is we mean when we describe something as fashionable, particularly since fashion (and the fashion industry) is notoriously changeable and fickle – as Heidi Klum says in *Project Runway*, "one day you're in, the next day you're out." In their contribution, Jesse Prinz and Anya Farennikova argue that describing an item (be it clothes, music, furniture, or even ideas) as fashionable is to make a claim that involves appealing both to "the masses" and to a set of acknowledged experts (such as celebrities, fashion editors, and designers). The fact that an item appears on the runway is not sufficient to make it fashionable, unless enough consumers adopt that item – even if in a modified form. Likewise, the fact that an item is popular does not make that item fashionable unless and until fashion experts endorse it. Ugg boots were not fashionable for many years, despite their popularity. It was only when celebrities began to be photographed wearing them that they became a fashionable item and not merely a cozy pair of slippers.

Yet "fashionable" is not just a description of an item's status in relation to expert opinion and popularity. The concept of fashion contains two seemingly contradictory elements. On the one hand, we directly experience an item as fashionable – we just perceive that *this* dress is fashionable and *that* dress is not. On the other hand, we also adopt an objective standpoint and recognize that an item's status as fashionable depends upon a number of social factors such as expert opinion, as well as being relative to a time, a place, and a particular group of people – so we also know that this dress won't be fashionable in a year's time and won't be fashionable among, say, the punk subculture. As Nick Zangwill points out, this suggests that fashion involves two incompatible perspectives that create a sense of alienation – the first-person experience (we experience items as genuinely having the property of being fashionable), and the third-person objective standpoint from which we realize that fashionability is an ever-changing attribute that depends on social arrangements. We can't experience both these perspectives simultaneously, and so we are forced into an uneasy, and perhaps alienating, vacillation between the two.

This tension in fashion is something we are all too familiar with. Who among us has not had the experience of pulling out last season's favorite item of clothing – one that we thought was the height of cool – and realizing, to our horror, that it has entirely lost its allure. How could I have ever thought *this* dress was cool, we think? Or that I looked good in it? What was I thinking? Who hasn't cringed at those old photos where we (or our parents) proudly sport the latest 1980s hairstyles and power suits? The perception of fashionability that these items had *then* seems to be a kind of illusion from our perspective *now*. It seems impossible to reconcile these two aspects of fashion, and the tension that results, according to Zangwill, makes fashion an alienating concept.

On the other hand, we think that there are some people who are always cool, even when (or perhaps because) they do not dress in the fashions of the day, and who do not seem to be bound by the relativity of fashion to time, groups, and expert opinions. Being cool appears therefore to be a different attribute from being merely fashionable. Luke Russell argues that the property of being cool is an "aesthetic virtue," a virtue that he characterizes as involving caring about style and aesthetics for their own sake, rather than for the sake of appearing fashionable and trendy. The effortlessly cool person, unlike the rest of us, doesn't cringe when she contemplates her past fashion choices. The idea of "timeless" fashion, while appearing to involve a contradiction in terms, can make sense in

relation to such a person. Icons of cool such as Jane Birkin, Miles Davis, Humphrey Bogart, Kate Moss, and Audrey Hepburn have in common the ability to appear chic and stylish even as we recognize that their clothes are not or are no longer in fashion today.

Of course there are limits to the idea of "timeless" fashion. Fashions from the Victorian era or from Elizabethan times do not appear cool or fashionable now, no matter who wears them. Indeed, it is interesting to consider whether the concept of "cool" can be applied to historical eras in which fashion is constrained by social and gender conventions to a far greater degree than is the case in most modern liberal societies. It's hard to imagine a woman dressed in Jane Austen-era clothes as "cool," even though she might be fashionable given the standards of the time. Historical figures who might qualify as "cool," such as Lord Byron, are individuals who had a degree of financial and/or social freedom (usually arising from wealth and leisure) that allowed them to exercise their aesthetic choices in a way that was not possible for individuals who were more constrained by convention and circumstance. Perhaps, then, being cool is also a matter of having freedom to exercise one's tastes, and the resources to be able to do this.

Fashion, Style, and Design

Fashion is also closely connected to style and design more broadly. Andy Hamilton addresses the debate between those who believe that design (whether of furniture, clothes, buildings, and household appliances) should primarily be driven by considerations of function, and those who believe that design must also be guided by aesthetic considerations. The close connection between fashion and other areas of design is evident from the numerous collaborations between fashion designers and the design of household furniture and appliances. Calvin Klein and Laura Ashley are just two designers who have also produced designs in furnishings, bed linen, and homewares as well as clothing, and the fashion house Versace has collaborated on not only the architecture of a hotel (The Palazzo Versace hotel chain) but also on the design of every aspect of the hotel rooms and lobby. Even without explicit collaborations between fashion designers and architects and industrial design, there is a strong interconnection between fashion and the aesthetic of an era. This can be hard to see in relation to our own time, when developments in

Strongs connected Fashion aesthetic

contemporary fashion can seem isolated from developments in technology, science, and design more broadly. But when we see TV shows such as *Mad Men* (set in 1960s New York City) and HBO's *Boardwalk Empire* (set in Atlantic City in the 1920s) it is clear that part of the recreation of the eras in those shows involves recreating a total aesthetic – not just the clothes that people wore, but every aspect of their lives and the world they inhabit. In these shows, as well as in movies such as *LA Confidential* (1950s) and *The Ice Storm* (1970s), we clearly see the interconnection between fashion and almost every aspect of everyday life – office design, car design, architecture, household items, appliances, and furnishings. This help us to see how fashion integrates with design, and to understand how fashion can qualify as having an aesthetic status equal to that of architecture and industrial and household design. We can't isolate fashion in dress from fashion in other areas of design, and since many see architecture and industrial design as topics worthy of serious aesthetic consideration, it becomes apparent that fashion in dress is equally important as a subject.   *— Fashion effects values, way of life, employment*

The idea of fashion as a part of the total aesthetic of a particular time and culture also explains why there is such a strong connection between fashion and fantasy. Fashion and fashion design present us with not only choices in what we can wear and how we present ourselves to others, but can represent whole lifestyles. The connection between fashion and fantasy is obvious in fashion advertising – where fashions are depicted in such a way as to evoke particular values, ways of life, even kinds of employment. Michael Kors' recent advertising campaigns, for example, depict an elegant woman being photographed on the red carpet, exiting a luxurious car, and walking with an equally elegant man through the snow. These images create the illusion of a life of wealth, fame, and privilege – the details of the clothes themselves are almost secondary to this aura. The connection between fashion and fantasy is particularly evident in the collaborations between fashion designers and the perfume industry. Cynthia Freeland explores this connection in her chapter, highlighting the seductive nature of much perfume advertising. The long, intricate stories told in Chanel's recent perfume ads are almost mini-movies, involving distinct characters, intricate plots, mystery, and romance. Since the viewer is unable to experience the perfume directly, these ads convey the *idea* of the perfume – the idea of the kind of woman who wears it, rather than attempting to describe the scent itself.

Wealth, fame, privilege

Ada Brunstein reveals another side to the relationship between fashion and design. She explores the integration of technology and fashion, and demonstrates how wider social changes in communication technology are incorporated into what we wear in new and exciting ways. Our clothes might, in the not too distant future, be able to receive and send messages to other people, depict changing images, and impart sensations (such as the sensation of being hugged). This has the potential to alter our expectations of how, when, and in what manner we communicate with each other. Our clothes might literally, rather than just symbolically, express who we are and how we feel. This possibility, in common with other advances in technology, challenges traditional conceptions of what it means to be a person, and of how we draw the boundaries between the body, brain, and the external world, as well as highlighting and making explicit the intimate connection between fashion and identity.

Fashion, Identity, and Freedom

Clothing ourselves is clearly not simply a matter of what is convenient or comfortable. It is also not just a matter of what is fashionable this year (since a wide variety of styles may meet that criterion) or of what looks good on us. What we wear communicates many different messages to those around us. Fashion can be important as a way of expressing our personal style, our preferences, and even our moods. As Daniel Yim explains, fashion is one of the primary ways we have of exercising our autonomy and freedom of expression. Indeed, he explains, freedom of expression is seen as a central value of liberal societies such as the United States, so much so that in some cases courts have ruled that it is a violation of students' rights to freedom of expression to require them to wear school uniforms.

Of course fashion is not always or even primarily about individuality. As Yim points out, it is also a powerful means of communicating group membership and social roles. The clothes we wear, along with hairstyles and other items of adornment, can and often do, whether we are aware of it or not, communicate our social and professional roles and status – think power dressing, fitness freaks, ladies who lunch. They may also communicate our gender, our sexuality, our political commitments, our religious and moral beliefs, and our aesthetic judgments. If you are unconvinced, consider the fact that people who hold conservative religious views tend also to dress very conservatively – modest clothing that is conventional can therefore reveal important information about

  JESSICA WOLFENDALE AND JEANETTE KENNETT

certain of the wearer's moral and religious commitments, as well as their attitude toward sexual modesty and behavior and gender roles.

We think uniforms provide further insight into the connection between clothing, style and social identity. Military and police uniforms are designed explicitly to generate solidarity among military and police personnel, and to communicate to outsiders the status and authority of those who wear those uniforms. When we see a police uniform, we immediately recognize that the person wearing it fulfills a certain role, has undergone certain training, and warrants certain forms of treatment (respect, for instance, or even fear). Other kinds of uniforms have become associated with sexual fetishes and fantasies and have reinforced traditional gender roles. This is particularly true of women's uniforms, such as those of nurses, maids, and flight attendants. Indeed, it's difficult to think a traditional women's uniform that hasn't been sexualized and fetishized. Unlike most men's uniforms, which typically signal authority and power, many traditional women's uniforms signify a sexually potent blend of authority and servitude. Nurses traditionally were submissive to doctors, but were in positions of authority regarding patients. Many female uniforms also signify what were believed to be ideal natural feminine traits, such as nurturing, maternal discipline (for example, nannies), and sexual status, submission, and a desire to please. This is particularly true of traditional nurses' uniforms and flight attendants' uniforms. Indeed, a number of advertising campaigns in the 1960s and 1970s explicitly invited viewers to associate flight attendants with sexual availability in line with the so-called sexual revolution. The National Airlines 1971 television campaign depicted a beautiful smiling female flight attendant announcing, "I'm Maggie (or another female name). Fly me." As part of this campaign, National Airlines requested flight attendants to wear "Fly me" buttons on their uniforms. Even at the time, a number of female flight attendants complained that the campaign was nothing more than a "blatant sexual pitch."[1]

Uniforms are also responsive to the aesthetic or cultural aspects of fashion. Female flight attendant uniforms in the 1960s and 1970s reflected the fashions of time, including mini skirts and psychedelic patterns and colors, and there were and still are a number of collaborations between fashion designers and airlines. However the advent of mass air travel, and changes to employment practices which ensure that a career as a flight attendant is no longer restricted to young, attractive, and unmarried women, has dampened the previously alluring mix of fashion, flying, and sex.

This mix of fashion, function and allure is also (perhaps surprisingly) found in military uniforms. Military uniforms have influenced consumer and runway fashion to a significant degree – trends such as khaki, epaulettes, braids, aviator sunglasses, and military jackets have been in and out of fashion for decades, and "military" is touted to be one of the top trends this year. Nor are military personnel immune from the influences of consumer fashion and from aesthetic influences. During the eighteenth and nineteenth centuries the British Royal Marine Corps wore beautifully tailored red jackets that, while certainly aesthetically striking, were hardly practical from a military point of view since they could be seen from miles away. Today, the Italian military police (the Carabinieri) are known for the intricate and ornate gold braiding on their jackets. In the United States, the Navy recently introduced its new Navy Working Uniform, which comes in a digital camouflage print in shades of navy and blue (there were already desert and woodland camouflage uniforms). Why? The Navy does not require blue camouflage – and so it is hard to avoid the conclusion that the pattern was chosen at least partly for its aesthetic properties, and not for military purposes. As this and the earlier examples indicate, fashion cannot be separated from the broader socio-cultural context. Fashion reveals and expresses the zeitgeist of the time, a theme taken up by a number of our contributors.

It is precisely because fashion can exemplify prevailing cultural, moral, and political norms that those who reject conventional norms typically express their rejection through their clothes and adornments, among other means. Sub-cultures such as hippies, emos, Goths, and punks are identified not just by their dress but also by the set of moral and political beliefs those clothes are taken to represent. In addition, fashion can play an extremely important role in political and social recognition of marginalized groups. Samantha Brennan explores how important it is that ways of dressing that communicate sexual preference to others be both recognized and accepted by the community in order for homosexual and bisexual men and women to be recognized as such by their communities (and thus for them to achieve equal visibility). Daniel Yim argues that fashion can be an extremely powerful political statement, raising complex ideas about justice, solidarity, and morality. The image of Tommie Smith and John Carlos raising black-gloved hands in the air at the 1968 Summer Olympics remains one of the central images symbolizing solidarity and political activism among members of an oppressed community. And both Brennan and Yim highlight the role that fashion can have as an important means of self-expression and assertion of sexual status and identity for people with a disability.

Fashion is therefore a central part of not only how we self-identify, but also how we identify ourselves to others in our community and how

JESSICA WOLFENDALE AND JEANETTE KENNETT

we express important political ideas about group identification, solidarity, equality, and justice. To dismiss fashion as legitimate topic for philosophical analysis is to miss this important connection.

Yet, while fashion can be both liberating and a valuable means of self-expression, fashion has also been associated with repression and control. For women in particular, fashion can be literally restricting. As Rae Langton and Lauren Ashwell argue, women's fashions often physically restrict women's movements. This is obvious in historical fashions such as foot binding in China and corsets in Victorian England, but it is still prevalent in modern women's fashions. One cannot run in high heels and pencil skirts, and norms of modesty affect women far more than they do men – women must monitor whether their blouses are too low cut and their skirts too short – and such self-censorship can restrict physical movement and freedom as effectively as heels and tight skirts. This aspect of fashion suggests that fashion has a dark side – and so (for women at least) to pay attention to fashion is to be enslaved to fashion – to be forced to engage in a practice that is, even at its most benign, a restriction on autonomy.

It does seem clear that fashion as a practice affects women more than men, often in negative ways, and is one that girls are socialized into at increasingly early ages. Louise Collins focuses on the role of fashion dolls, notably Barbie dolls, in instilling a gendered preoccupation with fashion, body shape, and appearance. Her critical analysis reveals how young girls are instructed in the correct ways to play with Barbie. As she says, "In adorning and posing Barbie the girl rehearses the gestures and rituals of embodied femininity to be used in grooming her future adult self." Barbie play instills norms of attractiveness, suggests suitably feminine careers and pastimes, and importantly prepares the child for her role as consumer. Indeed it is largely through the success of fashion toys such as Barbie that children have acquired value as consumers in their own right, a development that raises a host of ethical issues surrounding marketing, gender stereotyping, and the sexualization of children.

Can We Be Ethical *and* Fashionable?

There is another side of consumerism that is also ethically troubling. As consumers of fashion, we often fail to think about where our clothes come from, and who makes them. For most of us, our concerns about fashion focus on cost, taste, style, and wearability. Shopping is a process that can be fun, creative, demanding, and frustrating. Rarely, though, do we see shopping as an ethical dilemma. Yet, particularly in today's world, fashion is produced in ways that raise serious ethical issues. The ethical issues connected to the production of fur and other animal-based products are well known, but what is less prominent in most people's minds is the fact that most mass-market fashion is made in sweatshops by workers paid well below a living wage, in conditions of extreme discomfort and even physical danger. In their chapters Lisa Cassidy and Matthew Pierlott explore the ethical issues surrounding sweatshops. Cassidy adopts the device of an interior monologue to reveal and question the ways in which we commonly justify our consumer behavior – the processes of rationalization (well, I need a new sweater!) and justification (sweatshop workers would be worse off without their jobs!) that enable us to reconcile our desire for cheap clothes with our discomfort with the conditions under which they are made. Yet, it is very difficult to justify buying clothes that are produced in the appalling conditions found in sweatshops. The claim that economic considerations make it necessary to maintain poor conditions in clothing factories is one that does not bear close analysis – even if clothing companies passed the cost of improving factory conditions directly onto consumers, this would not cause a price rise of more than a couple of dollars per garment, surely a small price to pay to ensure a living wage and decent working conditions for those who make our clothes. However, for many people buying expensive clothes that are labeled sweatshop free or that are produced domestically is not an option (indeed such clothes just may not be available in many places) and so most of us cannot escape the dilemma by buying only sweatshop free clothing. Does this mean that we can't afford to be ethical?

Perhaps the working poor in the United States and in other countries where there is great disparity of wealth cannot avoid buying clothing produced in sweatshops. But the rest of us surely have a responsibility to do so, and by doing so create the market that would bring down the price of ethically produced clothing. A similar process has, after all, occurred in relation to factory farming – even grocery stores in small rural towns now stock free range eggs and meat. Thus consumer choices can make an impact on market behavior over the long-term. Moreover, sweatshops are not the only ethical concern connected with mass-produced fashion – such production also has significant environmental costs as well.[2] Thus there are strong moral reasons for practicing ethical shopping, and thankfully there are options for clothing ourselves that not only avoid

JESSICA WOLFENDALE AND JEANETTE KENNETT

Buying vintage

the concerns with sweatshops and environmental degradation, but are also responses to the concerns raised by consumerism. The surge of interest in recycled and vintage clothing attested to by the rise in the number of celebrities who wear vintage (such as Mary-Kate and Ashley Olson, CateBlanchett, and Drew Barrymore) and the popularity of online trading sites such as eBay and Etsy indicates that it is now possible to find interesting, wearable, and unique clothing that is both affordable (even for those on a very small budget – one of the coeditors of this volume once found an Armani jacket in perfect condition for $6), sweatshop free, environmentally friendly, and that does not add to the ever-increasing and extraordinarily wasteful amount of consumer goods in the world. Buying vintage and recycled clothing thereby enables the shopper to creatively experiment with the aesthetic pleasures of fashion without worrying about either the ethical cost of fashion or about being overly trendy.

The positive aspect of fashion is developed further by Marguerite La Caze, who highlights the many ways in which fashion contributes to our lives and provides a medium for us to develop and exhibit important social virtues. She argues that a taste for fashion is justified on both moral and aesthetic grounds. Fashion may be beautiful, innovative, and useful; we can display creativity and exemplify good taste in our fashion choices. And in dressing with taste and care we manifest both self-respect and a concern for the pleasure of others. There is no doubt that fashion can be a source of interest and pleasure which links us to each other. This sociable aspect of fashion along with the opportunities it provides to imagine oneself differently – to try on, quite literally, different identities – suggests ways of mitigating some of the ethical problems we have identified here. Fashion may cement friendships, express creativity, and be a spur to self-improvement and change.

Today, aspiring fashionistas have many opportunities to mix and match trends, decades, and styles. The exposure to ordinary people's fashion sense and creativity provided by internet sites such as *The Sartorialist*, *Style Rookie* (a fashion blog by 14-year-old Tavi Gevinson) and *New Dress a Day* (a blog by a woman who makes a new dress each day from thrift store dresses that cost $1) have inspired many people to become their own stylists – to break out of the conformist mainstream conception of what is fashionable and to experiment with their own personal style in new and innovative ways. This suggests that fashion has the potential to become more subversive, more creative, less conformist and less expensive. In the area of fashion, being virtuous need not condemn us to a limited, boring, or conventional wardrobe. It is fully compatible with style and fun. To which, as philosophers and dedicated followers of fashion, we say, hooray!

NOTES

1 "The Nation: Fly me," *TIME* magazine, November 15, 1971. http://www.time.com/time/magazine/article/0,9171,903213,00.html (accessed November 1, 2010).
2 See for example http://www.thegoodhuman.com/2009/11/22/the-environmental-impact-of-the-fashion-industry/ (accessed 8 December 2010).

PART I

BEING FASHIONABLE AND BEING COOL

CHAPTER 1

WHAT MAKES SOMETHING FASHIONABLE?

What Can Be Fashionable? From Pugs to Poodle Skirts

The word is, Montauk is the new Hamptons this summer. East Hampton is overpopulated, overrun by celebrities, predictable, and just tired. Montauk is largely unscathed and full of surprises. It is the epicenter of all things new and cool. There you will meet the new "It" people: emerging artists, young designers, models, and socialites. You will learn that taupe is the new black, that the trendiest drink is a new-style dirty martini, and that global scenesters are personalities *du jour*. The look is something vintage, something Green, the hottest tune is 1980s electro-kitsch, and the mood is hipster cool. The list goes on and is instantly updated.

Judging by this description, just about anything can be fashionable: people, colors, pets, ideas, artistic styles, places, and moods. Even political ideologies, scientific theories, and mortuary practices come in and out of vogue.[1] Here we will focus on fashion's most familiar form: clothing. But

Fashion – Philosophy for Everyone: Thinking with Style, First Edition.
Edited by Jessica Wolfendale and Jeanette Kennett.
© 2011 Blackwell Publishing Ltd. Published 2011 by Blackwell Publishing Ltd.

we think that the account we will develop may extend to these other cases. The question we will ask is, what makes something fashionable? To answer this question, we will use a series of thought experiments and real world examples to draw attention to the attitudes and activities that drive trends.

As we will see, fashion is not just a matter of beauty. Even bad taste can be fashionable (see Rei Kawabuko's recent work for Comme Des Garçons if you have doubts). And fashion is not just a matter of trends; a whole population can be unfashionable even if they go in for the same clothes. Nor is it simply a matter of what designers decree: Coco can be loco, Klein can decline, we can pass on Blass. What, then, makes one piece of clothing fashionable and another *faux pas*? Where's the magic? We will argue that trends and trendsetters both matter, along with attitudes, aesthetic affiliations, and contexts. The challenge is showing that each of these variables plays a role without overstating or mischaracterizing their respective contributions.

Do Masses Matter? Robinson Crusoe's Runway

1977 marked one of the most significant events in recent fashion: the launch of Calvin Klein jeans. The new denim code was clean, minimalist, and pure sex. The ad campaigns were provocative; the ultra-slim fit came as a revelation and the status of jeans as blue-collar was forever changed. The brand got an immediate cult following. Those away from the United States at the time discovered denim revolution upon return. Everyone was wearing Calvins. Everyone was talking about Calvins. Everyone craved Calvins. CK jeans were suddenly and overwhelmingly in style.

To learn that Calvin Klein jeans had become fashionable, all one needed to do was to look at the streets. Their huge popularity (over half a million sold in the two weeks following commercials) signaled that they were "in." Our methods have not changed since then. The masses are reliable indicators of what's fashionable at the moment. To find out what's in, we observe the pedestrians and visit street-style blogs. Once we see conformity to the trend by a large group of people, it is a sure sign that the item has come into fashion. Ultra-destroyed jeans, for example, are the prevailing look on the street this season, so we immediately conclude that the item must be in vogue.

ANYA FARENNIKOVA AND JESSE PRINZ

The masses, however, do not merely serve as a *barometer* of what is fashionable at the moment. Their role is larger. Consumers of the product are essentially involved in *making* the item fashionable. CK jeans did not become fashionable the moment Calvin Klein expressed his approval of Calvins' first prototype. Their "It" status had changed once their consumption statistics plummeted: everyone started wearing them.

You may disagree with this idea and think that we should keep the two roles of the masses apart. You may think, for example, that Calvins worn by a large group of people does *show* that they are fashionable. But, what *makes* Calvins fashionable are fashion experts – designers and editors. These people are the arbiters of fashion. They cause transformation of the mundane item into the one that's in vogue. The masses are like sheep – mere followers of what is determined for them in the fashion Olympus. Fashionability is always up to fashion experts. We just follow.

Let's test this idea by considering the following hypothetical situation:

consumption → sales → fashion

Stagnant Sales

Chloe has been an important designer in the last decade. Her collections are praised by fashion critics, sell out in major department stores, and spark rip-offs by mass-retailers. Chloe has recently designed a brilliant collection that even more exclusive designers like Lagerfeld would be proud of. It got favorable reviews and the upscale department store, Neiman Marcus, ordered most of the items. The collection, however, was ignored by the customers due to recession, and was eventually sent off to storage. Are the items in Chloe's collection fashionable?

Without consumers designs don't have influence

If the proposal above is right, then the answer should be yes: most fashion insiders would deem Chloe's work "true fashion." But, there is a strong pull in the opposite direction. We want to say that they are *not* fashionable. The reason for that is that Chloe's new designs have *no actual influence* over current fashion. Of course, her collection would have enjoyed success on the market, had there been no recession. But as is, the designs failed to inspire a following. Key looks from her collection never caught on.

No following, no fashionability. To reinforce this idea, let's go back to our real-life example with Calvin Klein jeans. At that time in history, to see that Calvins were in, you merely had to look at what the majority were wearing. You could very well ignore what was going in prominent fashion houses or on Paris runways. Had you checked on fashion houses, you would have learned that YSL had introduced peasant dresses and Valentino debuted his new obsession: a Goya red. Curiously, one would see no sign of CK jeans on the runway. Yet, which item was so obviously fashionable at the moment? Calvins!

Fine, you may concede, fashionability is ultimately up to the people wearing the trend. But why think that in order for something to be fashionable, the trend must acquire *massive* conformity? Can't something be fashionable for just one person even if no one else is copying the trend? Can there be individual fashionability? Enter Robinson Crusoe. Consider this twist on Swift's story:

Robinson Crusoe's Runway

> Robinson lives on an uninhabited island and wears whatever he can make from the materials at hand. One day Robinson looks at his soiled, nasty clothes and gets tired of his garb. He decides to construct a new leather jacket for the coming winter. Having planned the design, Robinson feels that he is on to something with the jacket. After it's done, he looks at it and decides that it is just the coolest thing ever. Isn't the jacket fashionable for Robinson?

Some may say yes; something can be fashionable for only one person. We think that this intuition is driven by the confusion between being cool and being fashionable. Coolness can be an individual thing. Robinson thinks that his jacket is super-special. It is aesthetically superior to all his clothes and has certainly raised Robinson's style quotient. However, the jacket would *become fashionable* only if many people copied it. To generalize, until an item of clothing is worn by a large group of people, it is just an element of *personal style*, regardless of how forward, cool, and exciting it is. Fashionability requires mass-consumption.

Do Experts Matter? Khaki Glory

One worry about the account so far is that it does not allow us to distinguish popularity from fashionability. To bring this out, let's consider khaki pants, which, until recently, were a major fashion no-no, despite their immense popularity. Khakis, we will see, are truly remarkable.

ANYA FARENNIKOVA AND JESSE PRINZ

Fashion-talk has a term "a basic piece." It refers to the items that constitute the fundamentals of style. Fashion-savvy people will recite to you a little black dress, a simple white button-down shirt, a sharp blazer, and great pants. These are the building blocks of the look. Like blank canvas, they set up your outfit for injection of color, diversion, and style. Here is a shocker: khakis are not on the fashion fundamentals list.

You might think nothing could be more neutral, innocent and solid than a good old pair of Gap khakis. But khakis had been black-listed. They were not even "a nice try." They were a *faux pas*, causing fashion-insiders to wince. In other words, khakis were to fashion as Taco Bell is to Mexican food – an embarrassment.

That is, until recently. Khakis are having a serious fashion moment now. No longer are they a sad pedestrian obsession. These days, they are chic. They are relevant. They are even meaningful. Slightly rolled-up khakis, paired with an easy shirt, convey "urban cool." Worn with a leather jacket, they become "rocker chic." People who embrace beautifully tailored khakis are themselves beautiful, elegant, and yes, very fashionable. In summary, khakis did not gain mere sartorial recognition. In a matter of weeks, they pivoted from nothing to all in fashion: utter chic.

Why the change? It's not like considerably more people started wearing khakis. Khakis were already popular and didn't acquire much more circulation. That means that we can't appeal to difference in their collective consumption in order to explain their new "It" status. Neither can we point to a dramatic transformation of their look. The new khakis are nearly identical to their decades-old counterparts; those a professor would wear to class or children would wear to church.

So what *has* changed? Only that the key players – fashion insiders – have changed their minds. The players are fashion creators and its professional critics: designers, creative directors of the brand, editors, buyers, and critics. And their action? A declaration.

This declaration went through multiple channels. Established designers put khakis on the runway and in ad campaigns. *Vogue* and *Elle* ran khaki-themed editorials. Magazine exposure led to the production of khakis as a luxury item. Crucially, khakis went high-end without the involvement of conservative labels, like Ralph Lauren, known for perfectly executed classics. Rather, they were produced by the most coveted and forward brands like Dsquared2, Martin Margiela, and Comme Des Garcons. Having created a sensation in high fashion circles, khakis trickled down to the masses. Many interpretations followed, and khakis diffused as the hottest new item.

Who altered the status of khakis? Professionals, not the masses. But, didn't our earlier examples show that it was ultimately up to the masses to make something fashionable? This is puzzling. On one hand, when we determine what's fashionable now, we often just check on what the majority is wearing. On the other hand, we routinely rely on fashion magazines and the runway for their verdicts. Does our practice reveal incoherence? Who is fashionability up to: the experts or the masses? We believe that fashionability is up to both. Experts are integrally involved in "fashionizing" of an item by the masses.

Against this contention, one might argue that there are situations in which experts do not matter. Consider cases where a new look appears on street-style blogs before showing up on the runway. In fact, some looks come into style contrary to expert opinion. Here is an example:

Loathsome Leggings

> Rachel, whose style Rob always admired, shows up to a meeting in leggings. Eventually, leggings become a staple in her look. Rob is not a fan and desperately wants her to rethink her style. After mining the *New York Times* Style Section, Rob informs Rachel that many fashion authorities loathe leggings: they think that leggings should be banned to fashion hell. She is unfazed. "So what?" She says, "The trend is *major*. All celebrities are wearing leggings, and so is everyone at my work. Look around!" Are leggings truly fashionable?

We think yes; leggings are officially vetoed by the experts but are still in fashion. So, do experts matter for fashionability or not? As a matter of fact, they do. Once we consider how fashion cycle works across cultures, it becomes apparent that the role of fashion authorities is indispensible. Fashion is essentially a leader-follower culture: it is a large social institution that *thrives* on people following the lead. An even stronger view suggests that fashion-merit is a myth, systemically generated by the industry in order to legitimize designers' work. Brilliant designers don't exist. There is only brilliant marketing that successfully generates conformity.[2]

In summary, fashion may be considered fundamentally subjective and thus be solely a matter of taste, but it is typically the *experts'* taste that instigates a following. Were it not so, fashion editors would be out of jobs and American *Vogue* circulation would not reach 1.2 million. As of now, both have been vital for establishing and popularizing a trend.

ANYA FARENNIKOVA AND JESSE PRINZ

We obey the dictates of fashion experts about the majority of trends. But what about trends which are first born on the street or are disapproved by the fashion elite, like the leggings? These, too, acquire their "It" status in virtue of the leader-follower dynamic – only, the leaders in question are not certified professionals, but people with an intuitive sense of style, capable of aesthetic innovation: the trendsetters. We defer to the new authorities: models, celebrities, socialites, or anyone style-savvy in our social group.

Contemporary fashion is just as Kate Moss-driven as it is Anna Wintour-driven. In fact, the power of high-profile fashion personalities is so great that when a handful of them sports a new look, there is already an inclination to say that it's fashionable. On our analysis, it won't be fashionable until consumers follow the trend, but since trendsetters can be accurate predictors and causes of the trend, this way of speaking simply anticipates the nearly inevitable outcome.

The upshot is that we accept something as fashionable because people we *regard as experts* declared it to be so. This has been the case with the majority of trends. We embraced the new glory of khakis; the brave even went for cropped men's trousers and harem shorts (a veritable pants' liberation movement). But, we generally pull out when fashion gets extreme. Martin Margiela's coat made entirely of blond wigs, Jean-Paul Gaultier's crocodile overalls, and Louis Vuitton bunny ears seem beyond us. Extreme trends rule the runway but not the streets.

It would be rash to conclude from this that experts don't matter for fashionability. The fact is, such styles are a part of a completely different game. They belong to what fashion-insiders call "Fashion with capital-F" (or High Fashion) and so obey different rules. Haute couture (for example, Christian Lacroix) is artistically exquisite and most exclusive. Concept Fashion (for example, Margiela's wig coat) is fashion that is designed to express a specific idea: it provides a commentary on prior trends, or takes a bold stance on what is currently culturally important. Like Couture, its products are not meant for mass-proliferation. In addition, extreme trends may pop up in what is typically a prêt-a-porter segment. They are often put forth as suggestions: many are exaggerations that are intended to be toned down and reinterpreted, rather than used literally. They will not become popular (at least not in their literal form), nor are they meant to be.

Because capital-F Fashion works differently than mass-fashion, our general lack of deference to experts about extreme trends is appropriate. Experts have a full say in Fashion, but not in mass-fashion. In mass-fashion, they will tell us to take the trend to the streets; in High Fashion, the command is to worship.

Ironically – if our analysis is right – something can be a Fashion item without being fashionable. Recall the Chloe scenario. On our account, her collection is not fashionable because it failed to pick up a following. Still, many may have a lingering feeling that Chloe's work deserves to be counted as fashion. In calling it fashion, however, we merely recognize that the collection is a legitimate part of the fashion world, not that it is in style. A fashion item or a trend does not become fashionable solely in virtue of belonging to the industry (for instance, by being a part of High-fashion.) Instead, a trend acquires the requisite status *if* it gets "big" on the streets *because* some fashion guru declared it "the next big thing." A self-fulfilled prophecy, indeed.

Do Intentions Matter? Accidental Chic

So far we've been suggesting that, when it comes to fashion, many people must be wearing a particular style and that style must also have the endorsement of experts. But this analysis is incomplete. People also have to be wearing the same style for the right reasons. Mere convergence is not enough.

Consider the following case:

Runway Relief

> The latest, highly coveted Kate Moss Topshop collection is sent as humanitarian aid to a small island that has been hit by a tsunami. The islanders wear the clothes regularly, because their old clothes are in tatters. Are the islanders fashionable?

Our intuition is that the islanders are not fashionable. But notice that they meet the conditions set so far: group conformity and expert endorsement. The problem is, they are not wearing their wardrobes by choice. They are literally "fashion victims." Likewise, Nazi soldiers were required to wear designer uniforms manufactured by party member Hugo Boss, but it sounds strange to credit the soldiers with being fashionable, because they did not select these uniforms themselves. People are not fashionable if they conform to current trends without the right intentions.

One might think there is an easy fix. Perhaps something can be fashionable only if it is worn by choice. This is true, but even choice in not enough. Consider:

Coincidental Couture

Suppose that punk style is in vogue. Skinny jeans, flannel shirts, and combat boots are on runways and magazine covers. Then, by coincidence, a teenager in rural Arkansas who knows nothing about punk and even less about fashion goes thrift-store shopping. By accident, he picks out clothes that match the exact trends right. Is this young man fashionable?

Again, the answer is no. The accidental punk is *dressed* fashionably (his clothes happen to be right on the trend). But it would be undue praise to say that *he himself* is fashionable. He would deny the charge adamantly. He would be humiliated to discover that his lowbrow personal aesthetic aligns with highbrow fashion houses. He may be frustrated that people expect him to like punk rock, when he'd rather listen to country. To qualify as fashionable, our thrift-store cowboy needs to choose his getup for the right reasons; he must intend to conform.

The idea of conformity raises an immediate worry. Some fashionistas pride themselves on expressing their individuality through fashion. They want to stand out. This suggests that, at the very core of fashion, there is a kind of paradox. Fashion demands conformity, but fashion is also a form of self-expression, which seems to conflict with conformity.[3]

Fortunately, the paradox is merely apparent. Fashionistas are simultaneously conformists and individualists, because fashion always involves choice. First, the fashionista must decide to be fashionable; not everyone cares about couture. Second, the fashionista needs to decide which trends to follow; she might have a favorite designer or a preference for street wear over formal wear. Third, every day she must choose what to wear, and that often involves mixing elements and selecting something suitable for her mood, personality, and agenda. In these ways, the fashionista is expressing individuality and conforming at the same time. And, finally, she may add a personal touch that departs from current trends. If lucky, she may even help spark an innovation. Progress in fashion requires that innovators do something that isn't yet fashionable, and style mavens who modify trends may lead the way. Invention and convention are not opposing forces, but stages in an ongoing cycle of change.

Do Aesthetics Matter? Form Over Function

We have been suggesting that fashion involves a desire to conform, and that this desire does not preclude individuality. But the conformity criterion faces another problem. Recognizing that an item of clothing is worn by others and forming the desire to conform is not sufficient for regarding it as fashionable. Consider a case:

Gang Green

A local street gang has decided that green will be the gang's signature color. To identify themselves, gang members wear green caps and bandanas. Gang members want to wear what the others are wearing, so they choose to conform by wearing green. Are they fashionable?

Our intuition is that they are not. But why not? It can't be that the group is too small. As we will see in the next section, small groups can have their own fashion. Nor can the problem be that the gang is wearing green as a symbol of group membership. Demarcating group identity can be a major motivation in fashion. The problem seems to be that the gang is not wearing green on account of its aesthetic virtues. Compare the origin of the necktie. Apparently, Croats invented the ancestor of the tie (cravats, which derives from "Croats") when they served as hired soldiers in the seventeenth century; there were no uniforms at the time, so neckwear was used to signal national identity. Then, Louis XIV decided he liked the Croatian look, and adopted his own version, adding some royal flourish. The French masses soon followed suit, so to speak, and a fashion was born. The difference between King and Croat is that Louis chose cravats for aesthetic reasons.

This raises a question. What do fashion-conscious consumers seek when they select an item of clothing for its aesthetic value? A full answer to this question is well beyond the scope of our discussion, but we'll offer a few remarks. In fashion, aesthetic value is not the same as beauty. Ugly things can exemplify good taste if they have other virtues, like being humorous, sexy, ostentatious, distinctive, exquisitely crafted, or relevant. As we are using the term, all of these features are "aesthetic" because they go beyond function, and have something to do with form. Indeed, even when designers boast functionality as a trend, as in these tough economic times, they are really turning functionality into a form, by creating

ANYA FARENNIKOVA AND JESSE PRINZ

forms that reflect utility rather than, say gratuitous ornamentation. In the Bauhaus school of art, which helped to usher in modernist architecture, designers preached form over function, but what they really meant is that design elements should not introduce features that overtly exceed functional requirements. The Bauhaus was as aesthetically focused and form-focused as any other movement. Likewise, good fashion design is all about form, even when the aesthetic trend is to make form follow function.

Another important feature of aesthetic value is that it depends on the beholder. That does not mean it is a matter of *personal* preference. For an outfit to be praiseworthy, it's not enough that the wearer likes it. We can like things for purely sentimental reasons or because they are flattering. To wear something for fashion's sake involves regarding it as having aesthetic value that others would recognize. That's one reason why experts are so crucial in fashion. They can arbitrate what counts as good at any given time (recall khakis). Something once regarded as awful becomes awe-inspiring after we see it in a glossy magazine. Experts divide the gaudy and the glamorous – and they can even make the gaudy count as glamorous, as with Louis XIV.

So, when people choose a style for its aesthetic value, they are banking on the fact that it would be *endorsed as good by experts*. They are not simply assuming the style is attractive (it might be intentionally unattractive). They are assuming that the style is a good look, even if it doesn't look good. That is, they are assuming the style could appear on a boutique mannequin, or be selected for a photo shoot. There is no universal formula for what makes something good, because it's the essence of fashion that it values change. But fashion is an aesthetic pursuit, and fashion seekers will work to align their preferences with styles that would be recognized as praiseworthy by aesthetic experts. That doesn't mean a fashionable person is someone who consults an expert before getting dressed each morning, but, when confronted with expert opinions, fashionable people are likely to adapt their taste.

Does Identity Matter? Tribal Colors

On the story we have been telling, something is fashionable only if it's worn for its aesthetic value, and experts play a role in determining which things have value. But we also observed that being an expert is not simply a matter of getting paid to write fashion columns. Someone is an expert only if consumers defer to her judgment. This brings out a crucial fact about fashion: different groups defer to different experts. Consider the following scenario:

Mod-ist Mistakes

A twenty-something couple is obsessively into the mod subculture. They listen to mod music, hang out at mod-themed clubs, and, above all else, wear mod fashion. He's into narrow-lapelled jackets and skinny ties; she likes her mini-skirts, geometrical patterns, and androgynous hairstyle. These elements come and go in mainstream fashion, but this year mod is out. A style snob sees this couple on the street and scoffs, "That look is so last year." Are the mods unfashionable?

This is a tricky case, because sometimes the word "fashionable" is used to track whatever fashion gurus in top-line fashion magazines are recommending. In this respect, the mods may be woefully out of sync. But they are not making a mistake. They simply don't care about the authors of *GQ* and *Elle*. They defer to Townsend and Twiggy, and, relative to mod ideals, they are bona fide fashion plates.

Thus, what counts as fashionable depends on a consumer's aspirations. That does not mean anything goes. The mod couple could get it wrong. A thick tie would be catastrophic. The point is that "fashionable" is relative. When the term is used without mentioning a specific group, it usually refers to mainstream standards in the local culture. But, when talking about a subculture, we imply a different set of standards. Mods can be accused of making a fashion *faux pas* only when they violate the style standards of their cohort.

This brings us back to a theme touched on earlier. Fashion is crucial for group identity. It can indicate class, musical preference, religion, nationality, political party, or sexual preference. We are all very good at reading fashion codes, and doing so helps us make quick judgments about the people we encounter. If everyone followed the same trends, the use of fashion as social signaling would be greatly diminished. That would be a loss. Fashion is fundamentally tribal. It's a quick way of finding friends and foes, dates and dullards.

Some aspects of the fashion code are relatively enduring. The nouveau riche like conspicuous consumption, with a special emphasis on status symbols and labels. Those with old money are more likely to either dress down or don conservative clothes that look out of date to style trackers. Urban youth with few resources may go in for something garishly flashy. Bohemians tend toward eclecticism (such as mismatched socks) or wear clothes that indicate membership in a known counter-culture (such as punk or grunge). The working class will signal disinterest in fashion trends by keeping it simple, casual, and consistent over time. Religious and ethnic minorities will seek out innocuous styles that are readily identified with their groups or, if they want to assimilate, they will tend towards inoffensive mainstream trends. These are gross generalizations, of course, but they underscore the role of fashion in identity.

It follows from this that fashion expertise is relative too. Being fashionable depends on willingness to defer to mavens of good taste, but goodness of taste depends on group affiliation. Those who want to be fashionable must first identify the group to whom they want their couture to appeal. Only then can the appropriate experts be identified.

Does Timing Matter? To Everything, There is a Season

We've been suggesting that fashion is group-relative. It is also relative to time. Fashion is that it comes in temporally bounded trends. This might seem to be a merely contingent feature of fashion, but we think it's essential. Consider:

Timeless Trousers

Like many fashion-conscious denim devotees, Jeanette keeps up with the latest blue jean trends. She has pairs that are raw, destructed, engineered, and everything in between. But she also has one pair that seems to remain chic when every other fad fades. These jeans are so perfectly cut and so versatile that they strike Jeanette as absolutely timeless. Could it really be true that this perfect pair is always fashionable?

The answer should be obvious. No pair of jeans could be truly timeless. They have only been in circulation since the late eighteenth century, and in many places they are considered unacceptable attire. A woman in Sudan was recently arrested for wearing a denim skirt deemed too tight. Even Jeanette's "timeless" trousers are probably less enduring than she thinks; in 20 years they might seem hopelessly recidivist – likewise for her perfect black dress, and her all-occasion flats. Clothes that endure for many seasons, wouldn't survive a single century. Timelessness is a misnomer.

This is no coincidence. We think fashion *must* change or it will cease to serve its purpose. Fashion is used to signal that one is tuned in to trends and willingness to discard old robes before their threads wear thin.[4] A person cannot be fashionable without flux, and an item of clothing cannot be fashionable without being "in." The idea of something that is in fashion forever verges on incoherence, because the "in" implies a contrast; something must come in, and then go out. There are societies that wear the same fashion for ages (the Amish, for example), but that very fact makes them decidedly and intentionally unfashionable.

Fashion requires trends, and trends cannot endure too long without undermining the consumer's ability to advertise their awareness of the latest looks. In the contemporary post-industrial information age, trends have much shorter life spans than they did in the past. Major fashion houses introduce five collections annually: two ready-to-wear lines, resort, pre-fall, and High Couture. In addition, they often do capsule collections for "fast-fashion" chains, such as H&M and Uniqlo. Consumers feel compelled to follow such rapid shifts for various reasons: they need to adjust to weather changes; they want to signal that they have disposable income; they want to attract mates by showing concern for appearance, and they want to avoid the ridicule reserved for those who fall behind the times.

There are a number of factors that can influence the specific content of fashion trends. One factor is the economic and political mood of the culture. In conservative times, like the 1980s, we saw preppie trends and dressing for success.[5] In the freewheeling 1970s, the look was more DIY casual. "Natural looks" were popular during the sexual revolution of the 1960s, as were short skirts, echoing a trend of the roaring 1920s. Body types have also fluctuated with the times.[6] Just as richer people want to show control by looking thin, and poorer people want to advertise wealth by packing on the pounds, we have seen anatomical preferences, and accompanying fashion shift toward the dangerously skinny in times of economic growth, whereas more curvaceous looks came in after World War II to advertise renewed prosperity after times of hardship. Fashion has also moved in step with the women's movement. Women's suffrage ushered in the sexy, yet androgynous looks of the Jazz Age, and the women's lib movement coincided with Yves Saint Laurent's *Le Smoking*, a tuxedo suit that allowed women to hang up their party dresses and literally wear the pants.

Another economic factor involves the dynamics of class. In our society, the wealthy have higher prestige, so people with less often imitate the looks of the wealthy, leading to fashion spread, but the wealthy want to retain their elite status, so when the high end fashion collection get copied by The Gap, it's time to move on.[7] Ironically, designers often come up with innovations for the elite by borrowing elements from small subcultures, which are not usually affluent, due to the growing democratization of fashion. Thus, an urban street look from this season might be quoted in an upscale boutique next season, then copied in H&M the following season, like a silent dialog between rich and poor.

Of course, endless novelty would put too much pressure on designers, and consumers who crave innovation may also gravitate toward the tried and true. Studies on aesthetic preference show that familiar things appeal.[8] This has two implications: innovations cannot depart too radically from what has come before,[9] and fashion will tend to repeat itself, bringing back styles from past decades. Fashion revival faces one serious constraint, however. If something comes back too soon, the wearer might give the false impression that she is out of date, rather than following the latest trend. Thus, overt revivals often come after a couple of decades when today's trendy young consumers would have been in their diapers. The fashionista who wore flared jeans in the 1990s was not wearing bellbottoms in the 1970s, so there is no mistaking her for a hopeless throwback. Recently, however, trends have been recycling more rapidly. This is a consequence of greater fashion pluralism, which allows people to shift between multiple co-existing styles, thereby avoiding the impression that they are frozen in a bygone era.

In these and other predictable ways fashion trends wax and wane. Each period has its own look, which both reflects the times, and becomes emblematic for it. In the history of fashion, we find the history of changing identity.

Conclusion: What Matters?

We have been addressing the question, "What makes something fashionable?" If we are right, four conditions must be met. First, a look is fashionable only if many people are wearing it. Second, individuals regarded as experts, though not necessarily fashion professionals, must endorse the look. Third, those who wear the look must intend to conform to the trend. Fourth, they must also regard the look as having aesthetic value, and this may involve deference to the experts. In addition, we argued that fashion is relative to groups; different subcultures have their own looks and their own expert-driven aesthetic standards. And fashion is also relative to times; what it is today will be out tomorrow. More concisely, a style is fashionable if it's a current trend that many people choose to follow because individuals they regard as chic give it the thumbs up. We suspect that this analysis could extend to fashion trends beyond attire (such as pets and pastimes), but we will be content if this helps you figure out whether it's time to shell out for a new pair of jeans.[10]

NOTES

1 Herbert Blumer, "Fashion: From Class Differentiation to Collective Selection," *The Sociological Quarterly* 10 (1969): 275–291.
2 Yuniya Kawamura, *Fashion-ology: An Introduction to Fashion Studies (Dress, Body, Culture)* (Oxford, UK: Berg Publishers, 2005).
3 Georg Simmel, "Fashion," *International Quarterly* 10 (1904): 130–155.
4 Simmel, "Fashion."
5 Paul Fussel, *Class: A Guide through the American Status System* (New York: Simon & Schuster, 1983).
6 Allan Mazur, "US Trends in Feminine Beauty and Overadaptation," *The Journal of Sex Research* 22 (1983): 281–303.
7 Harvey Leibenstein, "Bandwagon, Snob, and Veblen Effects in the Theory of Consumers' Demand," *Quarterly Journal of Economics* 64 (1950): 183–207.
8 Rolf Reber, Piotr Winkielman, and Norbert Schwarz, "Effects of Perceptual Fluency on Affective Judgments," *Psychological Science,* 29 (1998): 45–48.
9 Nancy Jack and Betty Schiffer, "The Limits of Fashion Control," *American Sociological Review* 13 (1948): 730–738.
10 We are grateful to the editors for helpful feedback and involving us in this exciting volume.

CHAPTER 2

FASHION, ILLUSION, AND ALIENATION

What Is It To Be Fashionable?

Clothes, shoes, hairstyles, ideas and activities may be more or less fashionable. But what is it to be fashionable? What do fashionable things have in common? It seems that if something is fashionable – clothes, shoes, hairstyles, ideas or activities – then those things must stand in relation to people who think certain things about them or experience them or engage with them in certain ways. Being fashionable seems like being famous in that it is what philosophers call a "relational property." If something is famous then it stands in a certain relation to people who know of it. And, similarly, if something is fashionable, then it stands in relation to people who think certain things about it or experience or engage with it in certain ways. Thus understood, both the notions of fame and fashion refer to social relations, and there are facts about what is and what is not fashionable. These facts are relative facts, but facts nonetheless. Presumably if a *person* is fashionable, they are so derivatively, in virtue of having fashionable clothes or shoes, or embracing fashionable ideas, or engaging in fashionable activities.

Fashion – Philosophy for Everyone: Thinking with Style, First Edition.
Edited by Jessica Wolfendale and Jeanette Kennett.
© 2011 Blackwell Publishing Ltd. Published 2011 by Blackwell Publishing Ltd.

Something may be fashionable in one group but not another. That does not cast doubt on the factual status of fashion thought and talk, so long as those relations are real. In the 1980s, Heavy metal rock music was fashionable in Eastern Europe but not elsewhere. "Hello Kitty" accessories are fashionable among young girls (especially in Japan) but not others. Post-modernism is fashionable among sociologists but not among (English-speaking) philosophers. Similarly, fame is relative to a group. One could be famous in one country or in one group but not in another. Oom Kalsoum was a famous singer in the Arab world. But she was not famous in the United States. Pugliese was a famous bandleader – among those who know Argentinean music. Toscanini and Furtwängler were famous conductors – among those who follow classical music. Quine was a famous philosopher, but (unlike Wittgenstein), few outside philosophy have heard of him. Similarly, things can be fashionable in some groups but not in others. Fame and fashion are also time-relative. There were very famous charioteers in ancient Rome that few have heard of now. And today's "celebrities" will soon be forgotten. Similarly with fashion. It was fashionable to wear flared trousers in the 1970s; but it was not fashionable in the 1980s, when straight trousers were in fashion. Behaviorism was a fashionable idea in the 1920s and 1930s, but no longer.

Thus fame and fashionableness both seem to be relations of something or an idea or an activity, to a group of people at a time who view the things in certain ways or who think or do certain things. (One person does not suffice.) Thus fashionableness seems like fame to be a sociological idea.

Appearing Fashionable

However, there is more to the idea of fashionableness, and in this respect there seems to be a difference between fashion and fame. This difference is the way that something can *appear* fashionable.

Suppose a man appears before me wielding a chainsaw and I am scared of him. I might describe him as scary. Suppose we ask: *was* he scary? Well, I found him scary. I was scared of him. But, while scared of him, did I think of him or perceive him as scary? That is not clear. I may think or perceive him as *dangerous* or as *wielding a chainsaw*. But it is not so clear that I think or perceive him *as scary*.

NICK ZANGWILL

Now compare fashion. In 1965 Mick Jagger, relative to viewers then, was fashionable. But he also *looked* fashionable – he *appeared* fashionable. Hence in the 1960s it would have been appropriate to say that he *looked* "groovy" or "hip," to use what was fashionable vocabulary back then. Or as they say now, he was "cool," in at least one colloquial sense of that word. What is significant is that these notions enter into the content of perceptual experiences of him. He looked cool. But it cannot be the sociological relational concept that figures in these perceptual experiences. When people represent Mick Jagger or his appearance as being cool, they do not represent other people thinking about him in certain ways.

It might be said that one can look famous just as one can look fashionable. Near where I live in Hampstead, North London, there are apparently many famous people – famous for being on television or in Hollywood films or the like. Perhaps some people have an air or aura about them such that one might think "I wonder if they are famous." One might think that someone looks as if they are famous even if we know that they are not. But this is different from the way someone looks cool. One *infers* that someone is famous or that they may be famous from the way they look. By contrast, a person looks cool in a more immediate way. One sees them as cool; one does not infer it from the way they look. So looking cool is different from looking famous.

Two Concepts of Fashion

I conjecture that what is going on is that there are two concepts of fashion, or two aspects of the concept of fashion; one is a sociological concept, the other is an appearance concept. The concept of fashion is schizoid – torn between two aspects, which are in tension. As in other more familiar areas of philosophy, when we reflect, it seems that there is a difference between first- and third-personal perspectives. (It is like consciousness in this respect.[1]) From the first-personal point of view, we find things fashionable and we represent things as fashionable (or "cool") in our thought and perceptual experiences, and that concept of fashion is not a sociological concept but an appearance concept. *This* concept may be expressed by "cool." But there is also the third-personal sociological notion. In the first-personal way of thinking, fashionableness seems to be represented in perceptual experience and thought as a simple property (that is, as a non-relational property), whereas on the third-personal way of thinking, it is represented relationally. We may experience fashionableness as a simple property, but we can also think of it relationally. Something can be or seem cool without being fashionable, but if something looks fashionable, in the non-sociological sense, then it looks cool.

This first-person notion of fashionableness is what philosophers call a "phenomenological" notion; it is primarily a matter of the *experience* of a thing, and only derivatively can we *think* of the thing in such terms. It is the other way round with the sociological notion; we can only have the appearance of fashionableness in this sense because we can think of the thing standing in the social relations. One notion prioritizes experience over thought in our understanding, and the other prioritizes thought over experience in our understanding. It is because of this first-personal aspect of the experience of fashionableness that it is not the same as mere popularity. People must do more than merely *like* a fashionable thing, activity or idea. They must experience it in a certain way.

Since I am making experience central, it might be asked: what about fashionable *ideas*? Intellectual life (including philosophy) is as fashion-driven as pop-music or high-street clothing. But ideas are abstract and cannot be perceived. Nevertheless, there is still a sense of "appearance" in which ideas can appear "cool," where what ideas seem, when they seem "cool," seems to be a feature of the ideas that is not a relation to people's thoughts or experiences. This appearance – what ideas seem – does not fit with the sociological relational concept of fashionableness. In intellectual thought there is something like intellectual experience, and ideas can have appearances in intellectual experience; in this way ideas can seem fashionable or "cool." There is therefore the same problem with integrating that appearance with the sociological notion as there is with fashionable clothes, shoes, and hairstyles.

There is no way to unite the two perspectives. Our notion of fashion contains a fault-line. The notion of fashionablessness is defective. Yet we seem compelled to think and experience in these defective terms. Indeed, it is not a way of thinking we can easily throw off. We might do so theoretically, but we would find ourselves deploying the non-relational notion of fashion in our perceptual and intellectual experience. We would still find ourselves thinking of things, actions or ideas as "cool" – that they appear fashionable in the non-sociological sense. But then we think two things that cannot be united.

NICK ZANGWILL

Fashion and Alienation

We both think and experience things in terms of fashionableness. From one point of view, fashionableness seems like a sociological feature of things, perhaps a complex relational feature of things – we think that many people of a certain sort at a certain time regard a thing, action or idea in a certain way. This is one aspect of our thought in terms of fashion. However, things also *appear* fashionable. People, clothes, shoes, hairstyles, ideas and activities may appear "cool." But in such perceptual and intellectual experiences of coolness we do not represent the complex sociological relational property. That would be untrue to the phenomenology of the experience of something as cool. Therefore it is difficult to fit together these two aspects of our common understanding of fashion – the sociological and phenomenological aspects clash. There is a tension in our thought about fashionableness.

What generates this tension is that a kind of projection takes place in our perceptual and intellectual experiences of something as fashionable, and what is projected flies in the face of the sociological conception of fashionableness. Is coolness a projection in the way that the faces that we see in clouds or the gestures that we see in trees are a projection? Not quite. For coolness is a projection that we are not aware of when we experience things in such terms. Faces in clouds are like the painfulness of nettles in that we know that there is no feature of the nettles that is the pain, and we know that clouds do not really have faces.[2] But the experience of fashionableness is not well thought of as such an imaginative perceptual experience. We know that seeing a face in a cloud is an imaginative experience. We can often will such experiences as we please. But the experience of finding something cool is not like this. We are not seeing something as cool but finding it cool. There seems to be a feature – the fashionableness or the coolness of things, ideas or actions – of which we are aware. So the situation with "cool" is not like seeing faces in clouds or gestures in trees, since we know that this is something we are merely imagining. Seeing something as cool is not like that; it seems like a recognition of what is there, and it seems not to be the experience of a relational characteristic of things, but of a simple characteristic of things.

The trouble is that we have only to think of our first-personal experience from the third-personal point of view to become alienated from it. For what we represent in our experience of fashionableness cannot be what we think when we deploy the sociological concept of fashion. For this reason, thinking in terms of fashion is a source of alienation, like that which Bernard Williams finds in consequentialist and Kantian moral philosophy.[3] (Given that thinking about fashion can be a source of alienation it is perhaps no wonder that fashion-conscious teenagers are so notoriously alienated!)

The Metaphysics of Fashion

So what, exactly, is the metaphysics of fashionableness? The metaphysics of fashionableness, I conjecture, is a mess! There is an element of projection in our thought about fashionableness, when something appears cool to us, which involves an illusion. Certainly, there is a tension between the sociological and phenomenological aspects of our notion of fashionableness. Nothing can really correspond to our notion of be fashionableness, for that notion is schizoid. My conclusion should come as no surprise: fashion is an illusion and a source of alienation.[4]

NOTES

1 See Thomas Nagel, "What is it Like to be a Bat?" *Philosophical Review* 83 (1974): 435–450; reprinted in his *Mortal Questions* (Cambridge: Cambridge University Press, 1979).
2 See Colin McGinn on imagination and perception in *Mindsight: Image, Dream, Meaning* (Cambridge, Mass.: Harvard University Press, 2004).
3 Bernard Williams, "A Critique of Utilitarianism," in *Utilitarianism: For and Against* (Cambridge: Cambridge University Press, 1973).
4 Thanks to Ryan Doerfler for discussion.

NICK ZANGWILL

CHAPTER 3

TRYHARDS, FASHION VICTIMS, AND EFFORTLESS COOL

A friend of mine who was about to go out on a date asked me what I thought of her outfit. Before I could reply, she added, "I want to look great, but I want to look like I made no effort whatsoever." These conflicting desires lie at the heart of the aesthetic virtue of cool. Many of us work hard at looking cool, monitoring shifts in fashion, carefully choosing clothes that are not behind the trend, that express our individuality while simultaneously positioning us within the privileged subgroup of people who are in the know. Yet many people who succeed in wearing what is fashionable also fail to be cool. In fact, trying too hard to look cool can be the very thing that prevents us from being cool. Genuinely cool people, it seems, are effortlessly cool. But what is it to be effortlessly cool, and how does it differ from being fashionable?

Being Fashionable

Most of us care deeply about how we are evaluated by others. We are eager to secure the approval of other people within our peer group, and often keen to signal our ambivalence towards the members of other groups.

Fashion – Philosophy for Everyone: Thinking with Style, First Edition.
Edited by Jessica Wolfendale and Jeanette Kennett.
© 2011 Blackwell Publishing Ltd. Published 2011 by Blackwell Publishing Ltd.

Typical teenagers, for instance, have an intense desire to be accepted and admired by their popular peers, and a desire to distance themselves from their parents and older generations. There are various means by which we can try to secure such approval and disapproval, including talking and acting in certain ways, but perhaps the most powerful and immediate means of doing so is by looking a certain way. We can control how we look to some degree by choosing which clothes to wear, how to cut and style our hair, and which accessories to carry. No doubt our aesthetic judgments influence these choices. For instance, my judgment that a particular cut of suit is elegant and flattering, or that a particular shirt is a beautiful shade of blue, can lead me to wear these clothes. Yet our decisions about what to wear are seldom, if ever, based on timeless aesthetic judgments that are divorced from a social context. What we choose to wear is strongly influenced by what other people choose to wear; that is, by what is in fashion.

What does it mean to say that something is fashionable, or that it is in fashion? It is obvious that the clothes that are fashionable now do not look the same as the clothes that were in fashion in the 1950s, and look even less like the clothes that were in fashion in the 1850s. This might lead us to think that, just as the word "gay" used to mean one thing and now means another, the meaning of the word "fashionable" has changed over the years. This thought would be mistaken. The correct view is that the meaning of "fashionable" remains constant, but that the facts about what is fashionable at any particular place and time are determined by the attitudes and practices of people who are in that place at that time. In other words, the truth about what is fashionable is a relative truth rather than an absolute truth.

What does it mean to say that truths about what is fashionable are relative? And relative to *what* are claims about fashionableness true? In order to get a better grip on the notion of a relative truth, let us consider the truth of claims that I make about what is to my left, and claims that I make about what is delicious. The truth of any claim that I make about "the person sitting to my left" will depend, in part, on where I am and which way I am facing when I make that claim. In this sense, the truth of my claim about what is to my left is relative to my location and orientation. The claim that a certain kind of food is delicious possesses a different kind of relativity. When I say that something is delicious, I mean that it tastes good to me. A claim about what is delicious is true or false relative to the tastes of the person who makes that claim.

It seems that there is some kind of relativity in the truth of claims about what is fashionable, but which kind? Suppose that I claim that black leggings are fashionable. It is not plausible that my claim is true simply if *I* wear black leggings or if *I* approve of people wearing black leggings. I might admit that black leggings are fashionable even though I think they look terrible and should not be worn by anyone. Thus, the facts about what is fashionable are not closely tied to my tastes. Fashionableness is not closely analogous to deliciousness. Yet it does seem that if enough people (or enough of the sophisticated and attractive young people) approve of wearing black leggings, and if enough people (or enough of the sophisticated and attractive young people) actually wear them, then it will be true that black leggings are fashionable. What is fashionable seems to be determined by what certain groups of people approve of and choose to do. As attitudes and practices change over time, fashion changes, not because the word has acquired a new meaning over time, but because the facts about what is fashionable are relative to group attitudes and relative to a location in space and time.

Not every kind of positive attitude towards an object can make that object fashionable, though. We speak of things being fashionable only in those domains in which there are fairly regular changes in attitudes and practices. For this reason it would be inappropriate to say that breathing is fashionable, or that eating is fashionable. Everyone always has and always will do these things regularly. In many societies for great stretches of time there have not been changes styles of dress. In such a society, some kinds of clothes might be judged to be inappropriate for various reasons – because they are immodest, or because they are too expensive, or because they look foreign – but it would be misleading to say that in this society some clothes were in fashion while other clothes were out of fashion. In contrast, in Western Europe after the Renaissance, attitudes and practices towards styles of dress fell into a pattern of regular change, and over time this pattern spread to many places around the globe. It makes sense to call something fashionable only if it falls within such a domain of regularly changing attitudes and practices. Many things other than clothes also fall into such domains. For instance, a kind of dance can become fashionable, as can a kind of cocktail or a particular holiday destination. In the 1880s it was fashionable to drink champagne and dance the waltz in Baden Baden; in the 1980s it was fashionable to drink margaritas and dance the Lambada in Rio de Janeiro.

Not every kind of cycle of attitudes and practices counts as a cycle of fashion, though. There was a sudden surge in the number of people who wore gas masks in Europe during World War I, but it would be misleading to say that gas masks became fashionable during that period. Nor does it seem right to say that emigrating to the United States became very fashionable in Ireland in the 1840s. Changes in fashion are not merely utilitarian, nor are they a matter of necessity. Rather, changes in fashion are changes that are driven by taste, which are freely chosen rather than forced. In light of all of these considerations, I propose the following rough definition: something is fashionable or in fashion in a particular society at a particular time if and only if it falls within a domain of regularly shifting attitudes and practices, and is approved of and chosen, not out of necessity or for purely utilitarian reasons, by a large proportion of the people in that society at the time, or by a privileged subgroup of people in that society at that time.

Given that this is what it means for something to be fashionable, it follows that it is fairly easy to figure out whether a particular thing is fashionable or not. All that we need to do is to notice an upswing of the right kind of approval towards that thing by enough people, or by the right kind of people. If plenty of people start dancing the Charleston (and they aren't being forced to do so!) then it has become fashionable to dance the Charleston. If we see that the models in *Vogue* have started wearing metallic fabrics, and that the party girls in the social pages of the newspaper have followed suit, then we know that the metallic look has become fashionable. Given that it is so easy to tell what is fashionable, we might conclude that it is equally easy to dress fashionably. For some people, however, there are significant practical obstacles to doing so. Some people cannot afford to buy fashionable clothes. Some people could afford to do so, but do not have access to places where they could buy fashionable clothes. Some people do not have a body shape such that fashionable clothes would fit them. For those of us who are not subject to these constraints, though, it is comparatively easy to dress fashionably.

Tryhards and Fashion Victims

In many circles, wearing unfashionable clothes is taken to be grounds for denigration or social exclusion, and wearing fashionable clothes is taken as grounds for admiration and acceptance. Let us call this socially entrenched practice of evaluation the norm of fashion. Given that the norm of fashion is so prevalent, and given that there is often a significant cost for those who fail to dress fashionably, we have a strong incentive to meet this norm. Yet some philosophers argue that we ought to repudiate fashion, in the sense that we should not evaluate others via the norm of fashion, and that we should not strive to meet it ourselves.

The most common philosophical criticisms of the norm of fashion are those that appeal to moral considerations. For instance, the fact that many people, through no fault of their own, are unable to dress fashionably suggests that it would be morally unjust to judge people based on what they wear. Moreover, it costs money to keep up with the fashions, and it might be considered selfish and impermissible to spend this money on trendy clothes, shoes and home wares rather than to donate it to a good cause. Some philosophers also argue against specific fashionable styles of dress on the grounds that these styles denigrate and disempower women, or that they prematurely sexualize pre-teen girls. These moral criticisms of the norm of fashion are important and deserve to be explored in more detail, but it is not clear that they provide us with a reason to reject fashion altogether. Fashionistas might argue that, just as we can admire and praise those who excel at sport without socially excluding people who are bad at sport, we can admire success in the realm of fashion while not socially excluding people who do not dress fashionably. Similarly, fashionistas could agree that we should not spend too much of our income on clothes, and that we should not sexualize pre-teen girls, but maintain that within these bounds there is plenty of room for the harmless and fun pursuit of dressing fashionably.

However, fashionistas must respond not only to these kinds of moral criticism, but to a form of aesthetic criticism. Trying to meet the norm of fashion leaves us vulnerable to being judged as tryhards, wannabes, posers, or fashion victims. These criticisms are familiar, but it is not entirely clear how they ought to be understood. I will distinguish three different interpretations of such criticisms, the first two of which are compatible with the norm of fashion, but the third of which undermines the norm of fashion.

The first way in which we could interpret the claim that someone is a fashion victim is to see this criticism as coming from within the norm of fashion itself. For instance, if Cyndi is wearing a flashy outfit that features prominent displays of designer brand names and last year's style of wide elastic belt, fashionistas might dismiss Cyndi as a tryhard, a poser, or a fashion victim. By this, it seems that they mean that Cyndi is striving to dress fashionably and is failing to do so. According to the fashionistas, Cyndi is a tryhard fashion victim because she looked to the wrong sources for guidance as to which clothes are fashionable. She should have been reading *Vogue* rather than imitating the styles she saw teenagers wearing in the local mall. Cyndi is a fashion victim in the sense that she tried hard to dress fashionably, but failed to do so. In order to avoid her mistakes, the fashionistas suggest, Cyndi should keep striving to dress fashionably, but do a better job of it.

The second way in which we could interpret the claim that someone is a tryhard or a fashion victim is to see this criticism as being grounded in aesthetic norms that are independent of the norm of fashion, but compatible with the norm of fashion. Let us imagine Candii, who is wearing an outfit that consists entirely of items of clothing that are genuinely fashionable, but who has combined those items in such a way that the overall result is a graceless mess of clashing colors that does nothing to flatter her figure. The fashionistas might dismiss Candii also as a tryhard fashion victim. By this, it seems that they mean that Candii is striving to dress fashionably and has succeeded in wearing fashionable clothes, but has failed to choose the fashionable clothes that would suit her, and has failed to wear her fashionable clothes in the right way. Even if we admitted that Candii has succeeded in dressing fashionably, it is clear that she has failed to dress well according to some timeless aesthetic norms regarding style and grace. In order to avoid her mistakes, the fashionistas suggest, Candii should keep striving to be fashionable, but should also pay attention to other aesthetic norms that guide the ways in which we combine and wear clothes.

The third way in which we could interpret the claim that someone is a tryhard fashion victim is more radical than either of the interpretations that we have considered so far. It is a criticism that undermines the norm of fashion, and thus would sound hypocritical coming out of the mouths of fashionistas who strive to be fashionable themselves. Let us imagine Allegra, who is wearing an outfit that consists entirely of genuinely fashionable clothes that are combined and worn in an elegant and flattering way. Moreover, let us imagine that Allegra wears only those clothes that are fashionable. She reads *Vogue* religiously, dreads the thought of being judged to be unfashionable, and hence never falls behind the trend. Nothing is more satisfying to Allegra than walking down the high street and being admired and envied by the women who correctly perceive that she embodies fashion. Allegra reliably succeeds in dressing fashionably, but the careful, studious effort that she puts into being fashionable can be the very thing that prompts the criticism that Allegra is a poser or a fashion victim. The problem with Allegra, we might claim, is that she is a fashionable tryhard, and that this makes her *uncool*. The solution cannot be that Allegra ought to try harder and do a better job of being fashionable, because it is her deep commitment to the norm of fashion that is the problem.

Effortless Cool

What is it for a person to be cool? We use the word "cool" in a variety of ways: to indicate a low temperature, to signal general approval, or to describe an emotional state or a person's temperament. Additionally, some people use the word "cool" as if it were synonymous with fashionable, and thus would claim that something's being cool is a matter of its being approved of by the relevant group in the relevant way. Yet it would be aesthetically naïve to think that a person can count as cool merely in virtue of doing and wearing what is fashionable. The word "cool" is also used by the aesthetically adept to pick out a much richer notion, a notion that I shall call the aesthetic virtue of cool. This is the virtue that we might refuse to ascribe to someone like Allegra, but that we recognize in people like Marlene Dietrich, James Dean, Serge Gainsbourg and Nico. The cool people on this list happen to be successful actors or singers, but neither fame nor artistic success is necessary for being cool. A completely anonymous, stylish stranger reading a novel at a café might, somehow, appear to be totally cool. A few of the well-dressed Parisians and Milanese whose photos appear on the website the *Sartorialist* strike us as being not merely fashionable, but cool.

Of course, there are some similarities between being cool, in this sense, and being fashionable. Being cool, like being fashionable, involves choosing to wear and to do certain kinds of things. Being cool, like being fashionable, is typically admired, at least by those who are in the know, and is taken by the cognoscenti as grounds for social acceptance. But cool people are not slaves to fashion. They have the confidence to break boundaries and wear whatever they want, and the skill that allows them to look great while doing so. Most importantly, the cool person seems not to have to try to be cool. Her cool appears so easy as to be effortless. It is Allegra's clearly visible effort to conform to the norm of fashion, and her fear of being judged unfashionable, that render her uncool.

Let us suppose that Allegra discovers that, while her back was turned, we have been calling her an uncool tryhard fashion victim. Perhaps she would not care about this kind of criticism, and would brush it off as the jealous remarks of pathetic critics who are not as fashionable as she consistently manages to be. More likely, though, Allegra would be stung by being called a tryhard fashion victim. After all, she does care deeply about securing the admiration of her more discerning peers, and fears being judged aesthetically second rate. This is what drives her to dress fashionably in the first place. It seems that the norm of cool trumps the norm of fashion, in that being cool is both more difficult and more admirable than being fashionable. We can imagine Allegra resolving henceforth to be not merely fashionable, but cool. Yet how could she achieve this goal, if one of the things that makes a person uncool is trying too hard? If genuine cool is effortless, would it not be self-defeating to strive to be cool?

Upon encountering this problem, Allegra might conclude that being cool is beyond one's control, and that, like beauty, it is a genetic gift bestowed on some lucky people at birth. If this is the case, then the reason that cool is effortless is that you cannot become cool by choosing to do certain things. You either have it or you don't. However, while it is plausible that we more readily judge that a person is cool if she is beautiful, it is not the case that cool is completely beyond our control. It was Allegra's actions and attitudes, not some innate, ineffable quality, which led us to judge that she was an uncool tryhard. Moreover, it is very likely that many people who are now cool were not always that way, but gradually developed from awkward, self-conscious teenagers into cool people. It is also plausible that some people who were cool for a period of time lost their status as cool because of actions that they chose to perform. For instance, a cool artist who sells out for commercial gain could thereby become an uncool person, as could a cool musician who attracts media attention, becomes addicted to the spotlight, and starts performing publicity stunts in order to stay in the public eye. Cool can be gained, cool can be lost. Allegra should not think that cool is inevitably out of her grasp.

Given that Allegra desperately wants to be cool, and given that she realizes that her own desire for social approval and slavish adherence to fashion are the things that prevent her from being cool, she might simply resolve not to care about what she wears, and not to care about how others evaluate her. No doubt it would be difficult for Allegra to overcome her deep aversion to the aesthetic disapproval of her peers, but let us suppose that she goes through some kind of Buddhist training regime and successfully ceases to care about her appearance. Would this be enough to make her cool? Are cool people those who do not care about how they look? The answer to this question, as to many others, can be found in an episode of *The Simpsons*, in which Homer and Marge quiz the kids about cool:

Homer:	So, I realized that being with my family is more important than being cool.
Bart:	Dad, what you just said was powerfully uncool.
Homer:	You know what the song says: "It's hip to be square."
Lisa:	That song is so lame.
Homer:	So lame that it's ... cool?
Bart and Lisa:	No.
Marge:	Am I cool, kids?
Bart and Lisa:	No.
Marge:	Good. I'm glad. And that's what makes me cool, not caring, right?
Bart and Lisa:	No.
Marge:	Well, how the hell do you be cool? I feel like we've tried everything here.
Homer:	Wait, Marge. Maybe if you're truly cool, you don't need to be told you're cool.
Bart:	Well, sure you do.
Lisa:	How else would you know?

(Episode: 3F21 Homerpalooza)

Bart and Lisa are right. Although not caring too much is one of the hallmarks of cool people, it is not true that everyone who does not care thereby counts as cool. After all, hobos generally do not care about their appearance, but this does not make hobos cool. The same could be said of high school mathematics teachers. It seems that being effortlessly cool requires not caring, not trying, *and* exerting enough effort to avoid the sartorial mistakes that are made by hobos and math teachers. Effortless cool appears to be paradoxical.

In light of this problem, Allegra might conclude that, strictly speaking, there is no such thing as effortless cool. Perhaps the effortlessness that we admire in cool people is merely the apparent lack of effort, and every cool person, deep down, cares about how she looks and abhors the social disapproval that comes with being behind the trend, and hence is trying hard after all. We praise ballerinas or divers for moving "effortlessly," but we do not really suppose that there is no effort involved in pirouetting on one's toes or scoring a perfect ten from the 5-meter platform. Rather, what we admire is the apparent effortlessness, or the concealment of effort that results in the graceful performance of an exceedingly difficult task. Perhaps this is what we mean when we praise someone as being effortlessly cool. Their aesthetic success *looks* effortless, and they manage to appear as if they do not care about the approval that it brings. According to this view, coolness is never anything more than an artful pose, in which effort is concealed from public view. Everyone who is cool is merely *playing it cool*, as the saying goes. In this case, the solution for Allegra is to continue to strive to dress fashionably, but to do a better job of concealing the effort that she exerts towards that end, and to hide her fear of social disapproval.

While it is likely that Allegra would seem cooler to us if she successfully concealed her care and effort, it is not clear that this kind of concealed effort is at the heart of genuine cool. In some domains, such as dancing or athletics, the revelation of concealed effort does nothing to undermine our admiration for the actions that we witness. When we discover just how difficult it is to dance like the ballerina or to twist and tumble like the diver, and thus realize that adept ballerinas and divers are actually working extremely hard, our admiration for their apparently effortless performance increases rather than decreases. This does not seem to be true of cool. If we discover that a seemingly effortlessly cool person religiously consults the latest fashion magazines, wants nothing more than to be admired for her clothes, and is terrified of being judged unfashionable, then we would conclude that she is less cool than she seemed at first. The genuinely cool person not only *appears* not to care about social disapproval: she does not care. The genuinely cool person not only *appears* to throw together great outfits without having to consult *Vogue* or slavishly conform to current trends: she does throw together such outfits. If Allegra is going to do more than imitate cool people, if she is going to achieve her goal of being genuinely cool, then her cool must not only look effortless. It must be effortless. This throws Allegra back to the original problem, though. How can she work at achieving a goal if one of the conditions for meeting that goal is that she does not to strive for it?

Self-effacing Goals

Perhaps we can come to Allegra's aid by pointing out that there are other cases in which the achievement of a goal is incompatible with the conscious striving for that goal. These are cases of what philosophers call self-effacing goals. A goal is self-effacing if our achievement of that goal requires that we look away from the goal rather than pursue it directly. Some philosophers have argued that the goal of happiness is self-effacing. We want to be happy, but if we deliberately strive to be happy, constantly monitoring our own level of satisfaction and asking whether this or that action will make us happier, we induce in ourselves a permanently unsettled state of dissatisfaction. Yet this does not lead philosophers to say that the achievement of happiness is completely beyond our control. The recipe for a happy life, they suggest, is to pursue other goals, such as success in the workplace, artistic achievement, participation in communal activities, and maintenance of family relationships. Because of some quirk of our psychological makeup, the direct pursuit of happiness brings unhappiness, but the direct pursuit of these other goals brings happiness.

Similarly, there are some moral virtues that are self-effacing. We could define the virtue of compassion as the character trait that disposes a person to feel appropriate distress at the suffering experienced by others. A person who is compassionate is for that reason morally admirable to some degree, which is just another way of saying that compassion is a moral virtue. Yet our awareness of the fact that people are admired for their compassion can provide us with a less than admirable motive for being compassionate ourselves: we might strive to be compassionate in the hope that we will be admired for our virtue. Someone who strives directly to be compassionate is less admirable than someone for whom compassion is natural and easy. The genuinely compassionate person, it seems, is she who is moved directly by the suffering of others and not by a desire that she be seen to be compassionate herself.

Why is it more admirable to be compassionate without consciously striving to be compassionate, and less admirable to be studiously compassionate? Giving a complete answer to this question would require a lengthy detour into the philosophical territory known as virtue ethics. Let us instead briefly note two points. First, we should note that morality is *other-directed* rather than self-directed. Morality asks that we value other people in and of themselves, not merely as a means to securing our own happiness. Hence, the person who tries to be virtuous in order that she be admired is not valuing what morally ought to be valued. Even if she is doing the right thing, she is doing it for the wrong kind of reason. In contrast, the genuinely virtuous person cares directly for the wellbeing of others, and it is this direct care that makes her virtuous. Second, we should note that moral virtue is a kind of admirable skill, and that doing the morally right thing for the right reason is *second nature* to the virtuous person. The virtuous person can see what is morally relevant in a complex situation, and is sufficiently wise to know what she ought to do. Hence, someone who lacks moral insight, and has to consult other people to determine what is right, is less than fully virtuous. In some respects, then, the fully virtuous person is effortless in exercising her virtue: she does not care too much about her own status, but is directly moved by what she should care about, and she finds it easy to know what she morally ought to do.

We have seen that striving directly to be happy and to be compassionate make us less likely to reach these goals. Happiness and compassion are both self-effacing, but for quite different reasons. The aesthetic virtue of cool also appears to be self-effacing. By striving to be cool we undermine our cool, and by slavishly consulting external sources such as *Vogue* and *Harper's Bazaar* we reveal our own lack of aesthetic skill and insight. So, how can we become cool? Perhaps the solution to this problem is analogous to the solution in the case of happiness. Just as we can become happy as a by-product of pursuing goals other than happiness, perhaps we can become cool by pursuing some other goal. But which goal should we pursue? At this point it might be useful to draw on the analogy with moral virtue. The morally virtuous person cares about the wellbeing of others in and of itself, and not merely as means to raising her own status in the eyes of the community. Perhaps the effortlessly cool person cares about aesthetic matters in and of themselves, and not merely as a means to raising her own status in the eyes of the community. She wears particular clothes not because they are fashionable, but because they look good. She listens to particular bands not because they are fashionable, but because their songs are compelling and they sound great. On this account, the cool person is the person who self-consciously achieves some kind of aesthetic excellence while not caring about the social approval or disapproval that she might attract in virtue of her aesthetic choices.

This account of effortless cool allows us to explain many of the puzzles that we have encountered so far. The reason that hobos and math teachers are not cool is that their lack of concern about social status is not accompanied by good choices in aesthetic matters. The reason that even Allegra, who succeeds in dressing fashionably, fails to be cool is not that she cares too much about how she looks, but that she cares about how other people will evaluate how she looks. Allegra lacks the admirable kind of aesthetic skill and independence that is at the heart of cool. What sets the cool person apart from tryhard fashion victims is not that the cool person does not care or try at all, but that the cool person's effort is not directed at securing social approval. The cool person is not afraid of standing out from the in-crowd. This kind of aesthetic success, it seems, is a goal that Allegra could pursue directly. By doing so, she might become cool.

However, it is not clear that this account of cool is correct. If the hallmark of cool is to achieve aesthetic success while not caring about the social approval that it often brings, then we could expect cool people to make their aesthetic choices in a way that is entirely independent of the tastes of the general populace. Yet it might be argued that cool people do not remain uninfluenced by trends and fashions. For instance, let us imagine that Allegra finally succeeds in cultivating a particular individual look and taste in music and has genuinely ceased to care about conforming to the trend or garnering social approval. Allegra now might strike us as being effortlessly cool. But what would happen if, upon attaining this status, Allegra is widely imitated, and her distinctive aesthetic choices become very fashionable? What would the cool person do in these circumstances? Would she be brave enough to stick with her choices, even though doing so would render her indistinguishable from the pack of fashion victim imitators? Or would the cool person shift to a new look, and get into a new musical scene, in order to throw off the pack and demonstrate to the world that she is not a mere follower, but is an independent aesthetic spirit? In other words, would the cool person be driven by a desire for social status after all? Would her seemingly effortless cool turn out to be nothing more than an act – a disaffected pose that is designed to impress?

PART 2

FASHION, STYLE, AND DESIGN

CHAPTER 4

THE AESTHETICS OF DESIGN

A few years ago, London's Design Museum witnessed an acrimonious dispute. The museum's chairman of trustees, designer-industrialist James Dyson, fell out with its director, Alice Rawsthorn, over her exhibitions policy, and finally resigned in 2004. Rawsthorn, commented *Sunday Times* correspondent Hugh Pearman, was:

a noted fashion aficionado, [who] put on a show of Manolo Blahnik shoes. Snipers cattily remarked that most of them could have come from her own collection. Then she famously decided to mount an exhibition of the 1950s flower arranger Constance Spry, clearing out much of the museum's historic collection to do so. Was that design? It was the last straw for Dyson, which is why he left.[1]

The emphasis on fashion, Dyson declared, was "ruining the museum's reputation and betraying its purpose. It's become a style showcase, instead of upholding its mission to encourage serious design, of the manufactured object."[2] The goal of the Museum, founded by home furnishings magnate Sir Terence Conran in 1989, was to "give a lead to

Fashion – Philosophy for Everyone: Thinking with Style, First Edition.
Edited by Jessica Wolfendale and Jeanette Kennett.
© 2011 Blackwell Publishing Ltd. Published 2011 by Blackwell Publishing Ltd.

the public on the difference between design as styling and design as intelligent problem-solving," Dyson affirmed.[3]

Rawsthorn eventually resigned too, and Terence Conran announced the construction of a new, larger museum on a new site. But as Pearman comments, the new Design Museum confronts the perennial problem of what design is:

> Design was always a broad church, and it is getting broader. It encompasses three-dimensional product design of the kind that Conran and Dyson are known for, also graphics ... engineering, posh frocks, home makeovers, even cookery [and] flower arranging ... nobody can really speak with authority for all of design.[4]

In similar vein, Virginia Postrel's recent book, *The Substance of Style*, argues that:

> Having spent a century or more focused primarily on other goals – solving manufacturing problems, lowering costs, making goods and services widely available, increasing convenience, saving energy ... we are increasingly engaged in making our world special.

She quotes the former president of the Industrial Designers Society of America as saying "We're seeing design creep into everything, *everything*," while graphic designer Michael Bierut remarks that "There's no such thing as an undesigned graphic object anymore, and there used to be."[5]

I'll argue that there is truth in what Postrel and Pearman say about the spread of design, but that it requires qualification and development. They are referring to two distinct trends. First, in the last 20 or 30 years the word "designer" came to be used as an adjective. Second, and much earlier, design came to be seen as a profession.

What then is design? Did it begin with a consumer society, or with the profession of design – or much earlier? Does it have to involve a process of styling for consumers?

My view is that design exhibits two sides: It solves functional problems, and it improves the look or feel of the product through style, decoration, and embellishment. Both these elements are fundamentally involved, and hard to separate. I start from the position that there are design classics, such as Henry Dreyfuss's classic black handset for the Bell telephone, or Dieter Rams's austere but very practical clocks, and other products for German manufacturers Braun, that are worthy of serious aesthetic attention – even if not of the order owed to a high artistic classic such as a Rembrandt self-portrait or Mahler symphony. It is of course important to consider, and to study, designed artifacts as commodities or mere objects – but not at the cost of denying the concept of aesthetic value, and of the design classic.

Design as Problem-Solving or Design as Fashion?

In today's popular consciousness, the notion of design as problem solving has become overshadowed by the notion of design as style and fashion. This is expressed in the concept of *designer labels*, which associates design pre-eminently with fashion.

Until the 1980s, "designer" described someone like Henry Dreyfuss or Dieter Rams, who designed appliances to solve particular problems. Today, "designer" is more likely to pick out fashion designers such as Ralph Lauren or Giorgio Armani who began as couturiers, but whose designer labels are now associated with exclusive products including clothing, cosmetics, perfume, handbags, luggage and home furnishings. Other designer labels include Gucci, Armani, Calvin Klein, Versace, Louis Vuitton, Dolce and Gabbana, Ralph Lauren, Prada and Chanel. With the post-2008 depression, designer label items appeared in discount stores, and affluent customers – those of high social status but motivated by the meanest of human aspirations, the flaunting of wealth – were alienated, and sought out new brands. A feedback loop of conspicuous consumption led to the appearance of new designer labels.

As a result, design is now often perceived, like fashion in clothes, as ephemeral by definition, something that rarely lasts beyond a single season. But although there has always been fashion *in* design, it is not by nature ephemeral. To reiterate, many early designs have become classics. The 1930s fashion for streamlining saw such classic designs as Walter Dorwin Teague's Kodak Brownie, and his service station designs for Texaco. Design had a practical function of lowering air or water resistance in Raymond Loewy's Pennsylvania locomotive design, or in Carl Breer's Chrysler Airflow, which pioneered design advances such as built-in headlights and a concealed trunk. Designer products can become classics because of their aesthetic appeal – the Umbra wastepaper basket's fluid shape might be an example – but functional deficiencies may prevent this. "Designer watches" are no more accurate than a Timex, and indeed the Movado watch is less legible. However some products are design classics *despite* functional deficiencies. The original Volkswagen Mini was a rust-bucket; Frank Lloyd Wright's houses leaked because of their flat roofs.

So we should reject the simplistic equation of design with fashion and styling without adopting the opposed extreme, that design is essentially problem solving with no intrinsic connection to style. Problem solving may seem to be what James Dyson does with his designs for vacuum cleaners. However, I would argue that his concern is not simply to find solutions to functional problems, but to find *elegant* solutions – the elegance is not just added on, but is intrinsic to how the problem is solved. Design is thinking about how we can achieve our practical ends with *style*; the Design Museum is not a Museum of Science or Technology.

There is no sharp contrast, therefore, but rather a continuum, between complex and simple problem solving, or strong and minimal attention to a design problem. The design of Movado watches and Umbra wastepaper baskets is largely styling. In contrast, the design of duct tape and brown paper bags, and – an intriguing example – Pierre Boulanger's unaesthetic but practical Citroën 2CV, is almost pure problem solving. As Witold Rybczynski explains, the 2CV's large wheels and soft suspension allowed smooth driving over rough roads; lightweight seats could be removed if bulky items were carried, or picnic chairs needed. If the sunroof was left open in a shower, rubber stoppers under the floor mats could be removed for drainage. The 2CV is neither a particular good nor a particularly bad design, at least not in the sense that the East German Trabant car was a bad design. But the creativity of the 2CV design is clearly a matter of ingenuity more than aesthetics. It might have worked well, but it lacked style.

In fact, it is not simply that there is a continuum between the practical and the stylistic. The most successful designed objects, whether chairs, cars, or office blocks, exhibit an interpenetration of styling and problem solving. The best-designed objects don't just solve technical problems; they do it with style. Problem solving in design therefore has an ineliminable aesthetic component. The Citroën 2CV, duct tape, and brown paper bags, despite their utility and ubiquity, are not design classics; Braun alarm clocks and Umbra waste-paper baskets are. So design problem solving is not just about ideas, nor is it a purely practical matter; one must be able to appreciate it stylistically, that is, aesthetically. To appreciate the Dyson vacuum cleaner as a design classic, one must see and experience how the improved suction-power has been achieved in an aesthetically satisfying way. A limousine car-door has to produce a satisfying click as the door is closed, and much design effort is put into achieving this.

The claim that design contains an ineliminable aesthetic component is open to challenge. We would all agree that changing the chemical composition of a detergent to make it more efficient does not count as design, even if Proctor and Gamble describe it so. But an extreme interpretation of modernist functionalism regards architecture and design as simply a kind of engineering with no necessary connection to aesthetic appearance or style.[6] Even a moderate critic of the view that design is intrinsically aesthetic may argue as follows: "Isn't the concept of engineering design one thing – and style another? The designer of car brakes, or of cams to alter the ratio at which moving parts rotate, is not necessarily concerned with the look of their design. Whereas a decorator who paints a wall viridian, that was once, vermilion is unconcerned with design-problem solving."

This line of objection, on my account, faces a dilemma. If there is an aesthetic element, one can talk of design; if there is not, one cannot. People talk of engine-design, and therefore, perhaps, the design of engine-parts. Where a part is hidden from view, it could be argued that there is no aesthetic component, and therefore that the part is not designed. But this seems false. Possibly, however, the fact that engineers do see the object (even if the rest of us don't) means that it does have a minimal aesthetic component, and therefore is designed.

David Pye contrasts design with invention rather than engineering: "Invention is the process of discovering a principle. Design is the process of applying that principle" – an application that, as I read him, is essentially aesthetic.[7] Consider the famous Dyson cleaners. These are cyclonic rather than vacuum-cleaners; they do not create a vacuum, but act as a spiraling wind tunnel, like a whirlwind. Hence they do not lose power as the void where the material is collected gradually fills up; vacuum cleaners, in contrast, become less efficient as they fill. The realization could have been botched, however – as it probably would have been if Boulanger, the 2CV designer, had had the idea. What is distinctive of Dyson products is their synthesis of innovative invention and stylish design – Dyson is an inventor, *and* a designer.

As consumer products, Dyson cleaners need to be stylish. In contrast, the Davy safety-lamp, which revolutionized coal-mine safety in the early nineteenth century, was a highly practical, functional item, not a consumer product. Sir Humphrey Davy was the inventor, if not the designer; and maybe there was no "designer" as such. It would have been inappropriate, for various reasons, to make it a stylish product. However, so ingrained is the human habit of good workmanship, that it was crafted beyond what was necessary for effective functioning. This crafting is what Pye calls "useless work" – a concept that I shall discuss later in the chapter – and it is a crafting that may count as design.

The Rise of Design As a Profession: Is Design a Response to Consumerism?

Earlier, I quoted the former president of the Industrial Designers Society of America saying "We're seeing design creep into everything ... There's no such thing as an undesigned graphic object anymore." What he means, I think, is that design is now produced self-consciously by professional designers, who have an enhanced social status. Compare, for instance, the status of modern "designers" with that of Harry Beck, who designed the London Underground map. Beck was a draughtsman, of lesser status than a "designer" of today, even though his map has become a design classic.

So when did this process begin? When did design become a profession? The *Grove Dictionary of Art* entry begins its discussion of "Design" rather late, around 1800, with the Industrial Revolution:

> [With the] move from craft to mass production ... the design process became separated from the making stage. This fundamental separation, which meant that a product had to be planned in its entirety before it could be made, gave birth to the modern meaning of design and, subsequently, to the profession of designer.

Grove argues that while Italian *disegno* and French *dessin* both meant "drawing," and in the early nineteenth century design continued to be associated with surface decoration and the use of historical styles, the modern meaning of design makes essential reference to mass production of consumer goods – a process that did not occur before the nineteenth century.[8]

There are two claims or assumptions made by *Grove* that should be questioned. The first is its interpretation of "design," according to which, design essentially involve response to a consumer. My thesis, in contrast, denies that "response to a consumer" is part of the concept of design (*Grove* in fact goes further and argues that mass production of consumer goods is involved; but even though exclusive clothes for a rich elite are consumer goods, by definition they are not mass-produced). What *is* essential to design is the duality of solving functional problems and improving the look or feel of the product through style, decoration, and embellishment. Whether the object is made in response to consumer demand is not relevant. *Grove* is right to cite "surface decoration" as one meaning of design; this is a distinct sense, and it bears on my theory in that it is a part of styling, although not all of it.[9] The finest designed products do not simply apply surface decoration to the solution of a technical or functional problem.

More on these issues shortly. The second claim or assumption that *Grove* makes is a historical one, simply in beginning its discussion around 1800.

Although design as such is not defined in terms of response to consumers, the *profession* of design clearly is. Authorities differ on when this profession originated. Postrel's twentieth-century dating seems to be supported by Peter Dormer, who argues that "The separation of craft and design is one of the phenomena of late-twentieth-century Western culture ... In the visual arts 'I don't want the craft to get in the way of my creativity' is a perfectly meaningful statement."[10] However, Dormer may be referring to the radical *divorce* between craft and design, rather than to the *distinction* between craftsmen and women and designers that arises with the appearance of the profession of designer. A nineteenth-century dating of the latter is suggested by a contributor to his volume, who cites the Special Committee of the (British) Council of the Government School of Design debating whether "the architect's art, or the art of the designer for manufactures, is truly a prosaic art" compared to the painter's "poetical" art.[11]

Others argue that professional design goes back to the beginnings of consumer society in the eighteenth century, which would associate it with other revolutionary developments in the world of the arts at that time.[12] As early as 1735, Bishop Berkeley, in his work of applied economics, *The Querist*, proposed an "academy of design" in Ireland to help perfect the manufacture of lace, carpets, and tapestry. The Oxford English Dictionary cites this as the first use of "design" to refer to the ability to improve the economic competitiveness of commercial goods through their visual appearance. John Gwyn's 1749 "Essay on Design, including proposals for erecting a Public Academy" claimed "great pecuniary Advantages, such as ought to engage the Attention of the mere merchant," in his proposal for improving training in the "Art of Design."[13] This project was realized finally with the founding of the Victoria and Albert Museum in South Kensington in London, intended as a repository of decorative art objects to inspire students of design – thereby improving the competitiveness of British against French goods by raising their aesthetic level. Wedgwood pottery is a classic early example of consumer goods of high quality, influenced by Chinese and Japanese ceramics.

Consumerism, Self-expression, and The "Invention" of Design

With the development of an early consumer society arose the concept of individual taste, as opposed to a homogeneous social taste with little room for individual expression, and its appearance preoccupied writers on aesthetics in the later eighteenth century. Charles Saumarez Smith argues that in England between 1740 and 1760 the concept of design in relation to a market of manufactured goods appeared, along with the independent profession of designer.[14] Smith links this with growing awareness of fashion and recognition that possession of consumer goods could be a statement of personality. The idea that consumer goods could be used to express one's character, social status, and personality can be found in Addison and Steele's *Spectator*, which offered advice to a bourgeois public about appropriate attitudes to personal display through possessions, including for the first time the domestic environment – furniture and interior decoration visualized as a whole.[15] As Smith notes, before the eighteenth century only the elite were "aware of [how] an interior could be arranged to convey messages about individual character and social status ... During the eighteenth century a much larger section of society began to have access to objects which could convey meaning as signs of consumer choice."[16] More people wanted to own goods that displayed individual taste, and manufacturers responded.

So was design, then, invented in the eighteenth century? The term, and perhaps the profession, was. But the kind of work that designers since the eighteenth century have done was earlier executed in a less professional and self-conscious way by makers of the object in question. We can speak of narrower and broader concepts of design. A narrower sense of design involves the formulation of plans by a class of designers, separate from producers, and which at some stage became professionalized; these products are manufactured, giving rise to consumerism. A broad sense of design, in contrast, involves planning in some form, whether or not by professional designers; consumerism is not essential.

ANDY HAMILTON

This distinction is implicit in Penny Sparke's very sane account:

> within the context of changing production methods [the designer's traditional] role became increasingly isolated from the "making" process, and ... crucial as the source of "artistic input"... while the design process itself remained constant, its parameters, within manufacture, became clearer and, in social terms, its application more widespread.[17]

This division of labor between designers and producers has parallels with the divisions of labor between composer-performer, and perhaps scientist-philosopher. Where the division was not expressed in the concepts of the time, all one can say when asked "Were there scientists?" or "Were there designers?" is: perhaps in a broad sense yes, and in a narrow sense, no.

Grove may be right in claiming that design in its *modern* sense originates when the design process became separated from the making stage, just as musical composition in its modern sense appeared with the modern system of notation and score, with its separation of composer and performer. A rise in status of the practitioners occurred with the appearance of the idea of a work of art and music, and of a *design product* in artifacts. But both work and product were present in a broader sense prior to this development.

Consumerism Is Not Essential to Design

Let's return to the question of how consumerism has influenced our concept of design. How does it fit in to the development of the profession of design and the meaning of "designer"? *Grove* is right to stress the importance of consumer products in the modern concept of design, but mistaken in suggesting that a designed product has to be one made for commercial reasons. It is true that design often has commercial ends, but this does not mean that having commercial ends is essential to the concept of design. Self-conscious concern with design in manufacturing may postdate the Industrial Revolution, but preferring one object to another on the basis of its appearance surely does not. What is new to the era around 1800 is the idea that such aesthetic and stylistic preferences can express one's identity. "Consumer," like "design," also has a broad and narrow sense. Where there are markets there are consumers – but it is only after the Industrial Revolution and the increasing dominance of market capitalism that one can speak of consumer*ism*, in the sense of self-expression through consumer choice.

Likewise, Smith and the Oxford English Dictionary are wrong to suggest that "the ability to improve the economic competitiveness of commercial goods through their visual appearance" is a meaning of design. It is an *application*, but not a *sense* of "design," just as "popular culture" is an application, but not a sense, of "culture."[18] The "consumers" of industrial design are factory-owners and industrialists. Conspicuous consumption in blast furnaces is unlikely – if an industrialist feels pride in having the biggest furnace, this is most likely because of its profit-making potential, not because of its appearance. Of course, capitalism is a crucial factor in the changing concept of design but my point is that design predates capitalism's advent as a world economic system.

To summarize my view so far: design has the dual purpose of solving functional problems, and improving the look or feel of the product through style, decoration, and embellishment. "Response to consumers" is not essential to the concept of design. In its modern sense, design allows for consumerism; but even this sense is not defined in terms of consumerism, but rather in terms of the prevalent *separation* of design and production, and the resulting professionalization of design.

We can conclude from the preceding discussion that design in its broad sense is still a quite specialized concept, therefore: preparations of a certain type for buildings, artifacts of certain kinds, and machines. When minstrels made up songs, and Schubert composed them, neither are said to have designed them. We talk of dress *designs*, but knitting *patterns* – dress designs are geometric or visual, whereas knitting patterns are purely algebraic or symbolic. Designs involve more than instructions for making an object – they involve artifacts or constructions where the visual or sonic appearance or feel is important. So explosives, plain paper-bags, duct tape, and glues are not (normally) possible objects of design, since how these objects appear is not important.

Were Neolithic Flint Tools Designed?

It could be argued that while problem solving and improving the look or feel of the product were involved in traditional pre-industrial crafts, we talk about early potters, body painters, and ax chisellers as "designers"

ANDY HAMILTON

only as a vague reference to their intentions and the fact that the results of their endeavors were deliberate. On this view, William Paley in his Design Argument for God's existence did not assume that God drew blueprints – just that he carried out his purposes or designs. He was like a pre-industrial potter or cook, producing by design simply in the sense of meaning to do.

In contrast to the more restricted definitions of design that have just been criticized, this definition is more liberal, and requires a careful response. There is no reason why Neolithic artisans would not draw or otherwise represent their projects in some convenient medium, such as in the sand or on wood bark. So it would be wrong to assert confidently that before the eighteenth century, there was no separation between plan or performance, design or production. It is true however that explicit plans and blueprints now play a key role in the modern sense of design, according to which design is separable from its implementation. The documents in the designer's briefcase are what we now refer to as designs. That said, it is quite possible for design, even in its modern sense – perhaps especially in its modern sense – to be subconscious; a designer might claim something similar to artistic inspiration in creating a successful piece of design, without making blueprints.

In its broader sense, the two aspects of design involve "care taken over appearance," whether through explicitly formulated plans, or through planning that is not expressed in a tangible form separable from the product. Separable plans and the notated musical score developed for similar reasons – because the intended structure had become too complex to be memorized and/or performed or realized by others. Without plans or scores, also, it is difficult or impossible to be original, to challenge traditional tastes or aesthetic norms, since originality requires the ability to realize complex and innovative ideas. However, in contrast to performing music, one can usually stop during the production of functional artifacts in order to reflect – as the early tool makers may have done.

There may be a deeper underlying issue here. Perhaps *Grove*'s claim that design originated in the eighteenth century rests on an assumption that we cannot speak of genuinely aesthetic intentions prior to this time. This view draws on the common misconception that the ability to appreciate objects aesthetically is the sole domain of the aesthete or connoisseur. This is a misconception because anyone can respond aesthetically to anything at all – not only to artifacts such as clothing, but also to qualities of rituals and public ceremonies, gestures, expressions, and so on – and people have done so since the beginnings of human society. As Donald Brooks comments, "Aesthetic discrimination and pleasure is probably found in all occupations. The carpenter delights in a good piece of wood, the mechanic appreciates a well-polished cylinder and the farmer a fat pig."[19] Aestheticism or "art for art's sake" – an attitude that developed during the nineteenth century – is not a necessary condition of the aesthetic attitude. The fact that objects we now regard as artworks were treated by the ancient world as essentially functional artifacts, does not mean that they were not aesthetically appreciated.

Consider a Greek – or ancient Chinese or Babylonian – craftsman working on a funerary urn. Some may deny that he (it would probably be a "he") is hoping to elicit a genuinely aesthetic response to the workmanship he is lavishing on the artifact; his aim is rather to appease the vengeful gods, and ensure a peaceful afterlife for the dead person. But why would the craftsman imagine that the gods would be appeased? The obvious answer is "because he believes that they appreciate beautiful craftsmanship" – an answer that assumes that the Gods, like humans, appreciate beauty, if not for its own sake, and thus have an aesthetic attitude.

Can We Avoid Designing? – The Idea of "Useless Work"

I referred earlier to the human habit of good workmanship, or crafting beyond what is necessary for effective functioning. This crafting is what Pye calls "useless work": "whenever humans design and make a useful thing they invariably expend a good deal of unnecessary and easily avoidable work on it which contributes nothing to its usefulness." Their crafting goes beyond the strictly functional in creating ornament, excellent finish, and so on. The function of an artifact – what it is for – guides its form only to a limited extent and imposes minimal restrictions on creativity, Pye argues. Whether one is designing a hook, or a hat, an infinite range of shapes is available to choose from. "'Workmanship', 'design for appearance', 'decoration' … are part of the same pattern of behavior which all men at all times and places have followed: doing useless work on useful things." It is relatively easy to make ugly objects that still work and so "The essential bases of good design … are largely useless and, unfortunately, avoidable,"[20] Pye continues. Coat-hooks on a door could be replaced by nails and be nearly as effective; the charmless electricity junction box, installed by a 1950s Electricity Board in the

ANDY HAMILTON

street outside Durham University's Philosophy Department, illustrates the avoidability of good design.

Many will regard Pye's concept of "useless work on useful things" as over-paradoxical. But is it really "useless" work? "Unnecessary and easily avoidable work" may well contribute to an item's value to its owner, as a conspicuous consumer – and to its practical usefulness if the display of the item makes the owner noticed and able to gain a coveted official post, for instance. Useless work is socially functional – we are social creatures, and we greatly value such work, as Pye recognizes. So I will re-label his concept of "useless work," calling it *directly functionless work*, work that does not help fulfill the artifact's *defining function*. The defining function of a table is to place things on and support them, for eating or desk-work. In Buckingham Palace a table may have purely decorative or ceremonial functions, but these are not defining ones if the object counts as a table. A ceremonial sword is still a sword; its jewel-encrusted handle is directly functionless, and indeed if it makes the sword hard to grasp, detracts from its defining function of injuring and killing one's enemies, just as much as having an unsharpened blade would.

There is a beautifully knapped stone ax exhibited in the British Museum, which according to experts is too large to be effective in cutting up meat and so forth, and was probably designed as a status symbol. It may be a good status symbol, but though arguably designed, is not a good example of its defining function.

The Function and Value of Fashion

Finally, we turn to the status of fashion itself, and the connection between the preceding account of design, and fashion design in clothes. Most fashion design is at the opposite end of the spectrum from problem solving in Dyson's sense, though there is clothing that is designed to serve specific functions for specialized occupations such as astronauts, deep sea divers, or crime scene investigators that owes something to fashion and much to problem solving. But it would be wrong to assume that in fashion, design problems have mostly been solved. With new constraints and opportunities on material, shape, size and ease of assembly, new design problems arise.

Someone who was concerned only with style and not at all with design as problem solving or high art might be argued to be aesthetically impoverished. But the opposite may also be true. As I argued earlier, directly functionless work – for example, the beautiful but not very useful ax in the British Museum – has psychological or social functions, notably self-expression and self-adornment. Tribal antecedents of modern fashion, involving personal adornment, were essential to tribal identity – every tribe would have its characteristic appearance. With the Neolithic revolution, the appearance of agriculture and the later development of trade, fashion in its modern sense, which involves ever-changing styles and a search for the new, became possible. When cultures come into contact through trade or conquest, imitation of an alien culture can occur. (Simmel comments on the "widespread predilection for importing fashions from outside."[21])

It should be stressed that fashion design is an art at least with a lowercase "a" – a practice involving skill or craft whose ends are essentially aesthetic, that is, the enrichment and intensification of experience. And like other arts, fashion oscillates between expression of self and expression of society. One of the most penetrating analyses of this dichotomy is sociologist Georg Simmel's "The Philosophy of Fashion":

> fashion as a universal phenomenon in the history of our species … is the imitation of a given pattern and thus satisfies the need for social adaptation; it leads the individual onto the path that everyone travels … At the same time, and to no less a degree, it satisfies the need for distinction, the tendency towards differentiation, change and individual contrast … Fashion [operates] the double function of holding a given social circle together and at the same time closing it off from others … not the slightest reason can be found for its creations from the standpoint of an objective, aesthetic or other expediency.

Simmel points out that fashion's "complete indifference … to the material standards of life," can be seen in the way in which fashion arbitrarily suggests one kind of outfit as appropriate in one setting or time, another completely different outfit as appropriate in another, and, "something materially and aesthetically quite indifferent in a third … fashion is concerned with other motivations, namely solely with formal social ones."[22] Simmel would have in mind such arbitrary injunctions as this from *Vogue*: "Prepare to do away with crisp whites this winter: the new colours are flesh pink, café crème, oyster. The materials are as soft and smooth as the skin itself."[23] This arbitrariness applies to all conspicuous consumption, and thus much of design.

ANDY HAMILTON

In traditional societies, clothing has the primary function of marking social status and tribal identity. Modern fashion, in contrast, is often indeterminate as regards social ranking, but still serves as "social discourse." Under capitalism, self-adornment became commodified. Fashion is an industry, and its development – and that of the design industry discussed earlier – parallels the commodified art that succeeded the art of the pre-modern (pre-eighteenth-century) era. The process of commodification undermines the autonomy of the practice, in the following way. In the modern era, as Adorno argues, *autonomous art* develops when artists no longer work for specific patrons in church or court, offering in the market works that embody their own values rather than those of their patrons. But fashion can never be autonomous art – fashion designers cannot be solely concerned with producing items that reflect only their own values.

Fashion is design or decorative art that belongs to a genre that is essentially functional, even though its practical function may be masked by its social function – as it is with purely decorative furniture or ceramics, and ceremonial swords.[24] Humans would have somehow to lose the need for furniture, or clothing, before such items could become autonomous art. Even when exhibited in a museum, the functional origins of furniture or fashion in clothes are inescapable. Fashion, like furniture, has no option of pure abstraction; it always reflects the form of the body, and depends for its effect on being worn. Portrait painting, sculpture, and dance work with the human form, but unlike fashion, do have a possibility of abstraction.

Like sport and popular entertainment, fashion is divided into *classic and ephemeral* – or as it is more commonly described, the high and the popular. Fashion has its "timeless" classics (tuxedo, stilettos), and its less commodified avant-garde (haute couture), as well as the most commodified products (Primark, C & A, Wal-Mart). As in the high arts such as music and literature, there is cross-fertilization between these extremes. *Couture* is ordinary dressmaking; *haute couture*, founded in Paris by English dressmaker Charles Worth (1825–1895), is a design art where an entire outfit is created by a single artist. As Worth himself saw it: "I am a great artist, I have Delacroix's sense of colour and I compose. An outfit is the equal of a painting."[25]

I referred above to "classic design." But what exactly is "the classic"? The classic contrasts with the ephemeral. It includes high culture – the accumulation of art, literature and humane reflection that has stood the test of time and established a continuing tradition of reference and allusion, and which demands, and best rewards, seriousness and intensity of attention. But it goes beyond high culture in embracing all areas and social locations of artistic endeavor, and valuable artworks in all genres, including popular forms and functional arts. "Classic" means "excellent of its kind," and is eclectic across all cultures, "high culture," in contrast, asserts a hierarchy of the arts.[26]

There is a concept of "classic" that implies a living presence in contemporary culture. The tuxedo and high heels are classics in this sense. All music and art is of an era, and most is *only* of an era. But some of it endures, creating artistic tradition. I would argue that in fashion, in contrast, there are no traditions, just changing tastes – though fashion often seems cyclical, suggesting a reversion to past tastes.

Taste in fashion, like taste in any commodified item such as pop music, is mostly non-autonomous – even for conscious or unconscious rebels who wear the fashion of yesterday or of their youth. Yet true fashion does not involve following the herd, but anticipating them. By the time a style becomes popular, the true connoisseur of fashion has moved on. There is a creativity in the wearer's self-expression – a reflective activity, not a purely passive process. True sartorial or artistic individualism goes beyond everyday fashion by perpetually anticipating it, or by being timelessly hip or cool.

NOTES

1   Hugh Pearman, "London's Design Museum: the soap opera aspires to drama," http://www.hughpearman.com/2006/04.html (accessed October 23, 2010). An expanded version appeared in *The Sunday Times*, London, February 12, 2006, as "Something rotten in the state of design?"
2   Deyan Sudjic, "How a flower arrangement caused fear and loathing," *The Observer*, Sunday 3 October, 2004, http://www.guardian.co.uk/artanddesign/2004/oct/03/art3 (accessed 21 October, 2010).
3   Witold Rybczynski, "How Things Work," *New York Review of Books*, June 9, 2005, pp. 49–51.
4   Pearman, "London's Design Museum."
5   Virginia Postrel, *The Substance of Style: How the Rise of Aesthetic Value is Remaking Commerce, Culture and Consciousness* (New York: HarperCollins, 2003), pp. 8, 15, 17.
6   Edward Winters, *Aesthetics and Architecture* (London: Continuum, 2007), pp. 38–48.

7   David Pye, *The Nature and Aesthetics of Design* (London: The Herbert Press, 1978), p. 81.

8   Jane Turner, ed., *Grove Dictionary of Art* (Oxford: Oxford University Press, 1996), entry on "Design" by Penny Sparke, pp. 801–802.

9   Design in this sense – decorative as opposed to structural design is discussed, in relation to abstract painting, in Andy Hamilton, "Abstraction and Depiction: Paintings As Pictures," forthcoming in ed. G. Tomasi, *Sulla Rappresentazione Pittorica* (Palermo: Centro Internazionale Studi di Estetica, 2011), and available in English at www.andyhamilton.org.uk.

10 Peter Dorner, ed., *The Culture of Craft* (Manchester: Manchester University Press, 1997), p. 18.

11 Paul Greenhalgh, "The History of Craft," in *The Culture of Craft*, p. 28.

12 These developments are discussed in Andy Hamilton, *Aesthetics and Music* (London: Continuum, 2007), Chapter 1.

13 Charles Saumarez Smith, *The Rise of Design: Design and Domestic Interior in Eighteenth-century England* (London: Pimlico, 2000), pp. 118–119, 121.

14 Smith, *The Rise of Design*, p. 125.

15 Smith, *The Rise of Design*, p. 198.

16 Smith, *The Rise of Design*, p. 210.

17 Penny Sparke, *Design in Context* (London: Bloomsbury, 1991), p. 13.

18 A claim defended in Andy Hamilton, "Scruton's Philosophy of Culture: Elitism, Populism, and Classic Art," *British Journal of Aesthetics* 49 (2009): 389–404.

19 David Brooks, "Taste, Virtue and Class," in *Virtue and Taste: Essays in Memory of Flint Schier*, D. Knowles and J. Skorupski, eds., (Oxford: Blackwell, 1993), pp. 66–67.

20 Pye, *Design*, pp. 12–13, 34, 13.

21 Georg Simmel, *Simmel on Culture*, ed. D. Frisby and M. Featherstone (London: Sage, 1997), p. 191.

22 Frisby and Featherstone, pp. 188–90.

23 Roger Scruton, "Aesthetic Education and Design," in his *The Aesthetic Understanding: Essays in the Philosophy of Art and Culture* (London: Methuen, 1983), p. 207.

24 This is not to deny that all art has *indirect* social function, as defined in Hamilton, *Aesthetics and Music*, Chapter 6.

25 1895 newspaper interview quoted in Marceau Simon, *Mode et Peinture: Le Second Empire et L'Impressionisme* (Paris: Hazan, 1995), p. 128.

26 Hamilton, "Scruton's Philosophy of Culture," discusses contrasting senses of "culture."

CHAPTER 5

SHARE THE FANTASY

Perfume Advertising, Fashion, and Desire

Scent is among our most evocative senses, but it also suffers from a relatively impoverished descriptive language.[1] Because odor cannot be conveyed through the visual format of magazines and television, fragrances must mainly be promoted instead through the use of verbal descriptions, music, and visual images. (Resulting verbal descriptions can become silly or inane, as with this one for *Bouche Baie* by Nez à Nez: "… our berries do the Indian swim and whisper marmalade stories in a bath of flowers.") Perfume is often described as *aspirational*. That is, a buyer wants to wear a particular perfume in order to borrow qualities of the person featured in advertisements. Perfume ads work by linking fragrance to lifestyle, showcasing luxurious settings and erotic scenarios. They also rely heavily on tie-ins with fashion and couture: classic fashion houses (Armani, Chanel, Dior, Gucci, Ralph Lauren, Calvin Klein, Missoni, Prada, Versace, and so on) are also major players in the perfume market. Ads for these houses' perfumes feature women dressed in the house styles, implying that the perfume-wearer will thereby gain the chic look of a particular design firm. Thus we see typical house designs in perfume

Fashion – Philosophy for Everyone: Thinking with Style, First Edition.
Edited by Jessica Wolfendale and Jeanette Kennett.
© 2011 Blackwell Publishing Ltd. Published 2011 by Blackwell Publishing Ltd.

advertising – knits and bikinis for Missoni, *haute couture* gowns for Chanel, lean sportswear for Ralph Lauren, and underwear or jeans for Calvin Klein.

Perfume marketing is carefully planned and expensive. Hitting the target market with the image of the perfume is all-important and involves staggering amounts of money. Perfumes are a $10 billion annual market with more than 300 new entries annually – many of which fail within just a year or two.[2] Perfume marketers stir up anticipation with magazine scent strips, video snippets on TV, and celebrity appearances.

Just as fashion marketing depends in crucial ways on a house's representation by the actresses and musicians courted to wear the brand on the red carpet at famous award shows, so also has perfume marketing shifted from using professional models to film or music stars as the "face" chosen to front their new products. The list is almost endless: Keira Knightley, Hilary Swank, Liv Tyler, Monica Bellucci, Naomi Watts, Britney Spears, Kate Winslet, Gwyneth Paltrow, Penelope Cruz, Eva Mendes – just to name the females. A good example is the promotion for Dolce & Gabbana's perfume Rose The One in 2009, which depicts the curvaceous Scarlett Johansson reclining against a padded rose-hued headboard. She wears a tight-fitting Dolce & Gabbana pink tulle dress, with one satin strap seductively falling off her bare shoulder.

My chapter will examine perfume advertising partly in order to trace changing styles in perfume fashion. My central case study involves comparing Chanel's distinctive video campaigns for its two signature scents, Chanel No. 5 and Coco Mademoiselle. Chanel's exorbitant ads orchestrate a combination of exotic settings, beautiful actresses, and handsome men together with fantastic props, music, romantic narratives, *haute couture*, and visual symbolism, to reinforce the message that the perfume purchaser will – in their classic phrase – "share the fantasy" of Chanel's chic style of understated classic elegance. Chanel No. 5 is a classic of the old school, associated today with the elegant mature woman who wears a Chanel suit and shoes. By comparison, Coco Mademoiselle is more trendy and playful, a scent worn by the younger woman who can toy with gender standards by donning a man's pinstripe trousers and bowler hat. We can examine these and other ads in order to explore standard associations between perfume and gender. Below I will discuss several examples of advertising for both male and unisex fragrances. In addition, I will review the rapid growth of perfumes targeted at non-Caucasian buyers, through ads fronted by Jennifer Lopez, Queen Latifah, and Beyoncé Knowles.

My essay is intended as an initial, rather broad consideration of some aspects of the aesthetics and ethics of perfume marketing. I will argue that perfume ads, however clever or artful, may not always achieve their desired aim. They can be cleverly constructed paradigms of ideology inducing consumers to "share the fantasy," but they may also induce resistance. I will close by discussing some of these, ranging from a range of blog discussions and critical reviews to various social network commentaries and YouTube parodies.

Chanel No. 5 and Perfume Fashions

Ever since the 1970s, Chanel has employed prominent filmmakers to create its ads, sparing no expense. It might surprise readers to learn how many reputable film directors have made perfume videos (either before or after becoming well-known). David Lynch directed a video for Calvin Klein Obsession starring Benicio del Toro and Heather Graham, as well as one for Gucci. Others who have made perfume ads include Ridley Scott (for Chanel), Sofia Coppola (Miss Dior Chérie), and Chris Cunningham (Gucci Flora). The role of creativity in perfume videos was recently recognized with the *Vogue* Fragrances and Film Festival, an annual competition launched in 2007. The phenomenon has even been granted the honor of parody, when Roman Polanski directed a commercial for the imaginary perfume Greed starring Natalie Portman and Michelle Williams, in affiliation with art dealer Larry Gagosian (who produced), with costumes designed by Miuccia Prada.[3]

Like fashions themselves, perfumes go through trends. Various decades have seen distinct tastes, from the 1970s ultra-potent smells like Opium, to the "clean" 1980s unisex scents like Calvin Klein's Eternity, and then from the 1990s heady patchouli-based gourmands led by Thierry Mugler's Angel to the cloyingly sweet "bubble-gum" scents of today. Amidst such vagaries of taste, Chanel No. 5 risks falling into "old lady" territory. Its complex notes are hard to "get" for today's teenagers who are inundated at malls by fruity-floral scents comprised of synthetic musks or rose laced with peach and black currant. To compete, Chanel has created fragrances targeted to a younger demographic, including Coco Mademoiselle (2001) and Chance (2002). Even the *grande dame* herself was given a makeover when Chanel came out with a lighter and easier-to-wear version of the classic scent, Chanel No. 5 Eau Première.

One commentator remarked of this new "flanker" product that, "instead of the elegant auntie that is No. 5, you get her niece, the Homecoming Queen who aspires to a career in public relations."[4]

We can explore these differences in perfume fashions across decades by contrasting the recent television ad campaigns for two of Chanel's iconic fragrances, No. 5 and Coco Mademoiselle. Chanel No. 5 is the best-selling perfume in the world, with a bottle reportedly sold somewhere once every six seconds. The fragrance was created in 1920 for Gabrielle (Coco) Chanel (1883–1971) by perfumer Ernest Beaux, and so named because it was the fifth of ten scents he made for her to try. Its composition includes aldehydes (somewhat sharp, bright-smelling synthetics), jasmine, rose, sandalwood, iris, and ylang-ylang. The prominent perfume scientist and reviewer Luca Turin says of this iconic fragrance that it can "refresh one's memory of what unalloyed luxury is about."[5]

Launched in Paris in 1921, Chanel No. 5 quickly became a success and it has continued to be popular ever since – sustained by the fact that the company spends an estimated $20 to $25 million a year in global marketing. Chanel was the first perfume company to do TV ads and among the first to use celebrities to promote its scents. Gabrielle Chanel, known for her witty aphorisms, uttered such gems about perfume as, "Without perfume women have no future."[6] Slogans for Chanel are similarly catchy, such as in, "Share the fantasy," "The spell of Chanel," or "Every woman alive/wants Chanel No. 5." The fragrance received a priceless endorsement when Marilyn Monroe said that it was all she wore to bed. An image of the bottle was immortalized by Andy Warhol for the seventy-fifth anniversary limited edition box in 1985.

To keep their classic No. 5 fragrance *au courant* and perpetuate its image of style and glamor, Chanel has employed a succession of film stars. The then-quintessential American girl Ali McGraw of *Love Story* fame was the face for the perfume in the late 1960s. The starring role for Chanel returned to its native France when the classic beauty Catherine Deneuve became the next face in the 1970s. She was replaced by Carole Bouquet, one of the "Bond girls," in the late 1970s and 1980s.

Nicole Kidman became the face of Chanel No. 5 in 1996 and starred in an extravaganza movie-ad directed by Baz Luhrmann, done in the style of their hit collaboration *Moulin Rouge*. The most recent of the Chanel mini-movie ads was done in 2009 by director Jean-Pierre Jeunet, starring his filmic muse Audrey Tautou of *Amelie* fame (she also starred in his movie about Coco Chanel's life). Tautou became the face of Chanel in 2009, replacing Kidman.

The Chanel perfume movies by Luhrmann and Jeunet employ mini-narratives of romance. Tautou's version is set aboard the Orient Express as it travels to Istanbul, where the star encounters a tall handsome stranger (American model Travis Davenport) in the corridor of her sleeping car.[7] The film is constructed around the theme of chance encounters, longing, and lost opportunities. Pent-up desire is fulfilled when Tautou returns to the train station after her tour, re-encountering the handsome fellow, who approaches from behind and kisses her neck. The camera rises in a swirling shot to reveal their embrace framed against the Chanel logo emblazoned in golden mosaics on the train station floor, while on the soundtrack Billie Holiday sings, "I'm a fool to want you."

This brief film required hundreds of people to produce, including artisans from Lalique who painstakingly copied etchings in the glass to re-create several cars of the famed luxury train. In an explanation of his interest in the project, director Jeunet comments, "This is much more than an ad. It's like patronage: a short movie financed by Chanel. I had complete freedom on the script. Recreating with pictures the emotions induced by a scent is an interesting challenge."[8] Tautou is suitably modest about her role as the new face of the perfume. She says that "it's a myth, it transcends all the women who wear it. For women, putting on perfume is the height of femininity. You wear perfume, you wear a secret. It evokes travel, discovery, secrets, mystery."

The Jeunet-Tautou film is less excessive than the Luhrman-Kidman commercial, which reportedly cost $60 million to produce (Kidman wore $41 million of diamonds in it). It made Kidman the record-holder for the most money paid per minute to an actor (she reportedly earned $12 million for it). Kidman has a close association with Chanel; she frequently wears Karl Lagerfeld *haute couture* for Chanel for her red carpet appearances, as well as in the film. The ad, set to excerpts from Debussy's *Clair de Lune*, shows a famous woman who escapes fans and paparazzi by leaping into a taxi where (surprise!) she meets a handsome stranger (Brazilian actor Rodrigo Santoro). They escape to his garret, but when duty calls, the celebrity princess must depart. The closing sequence features her statuesque back as she ascends the red carpet. She smiles up at him in his far-away garret, while on her naked back glitters a long chain decorated with the interlocking "CC" Chanel logo (made from 419 diamonds). The mini-film closes with his voiceover, "I will not forget her, her kiss, her smile ... her perfume."[9]

Several aspects of these two mini-films are worthy of comment. First, they feature a well-known woman who hooks up with an unknown man.

CYNTHIA A. FREELAND

(Santoro was popular in Brazil, but unknown outside that country before this commercial.) This facilitates viewer identification with the heroine and her fantasies of romantic adventure. The films emphasize female desire for the interest and attention of an attractive man. Through the perfume, the movies strongly intimate, such desires can be fulfilled. Kidman's character seeks an escape from the prison of her own celebrity; Tautou's seeks adventure and finds what she wants as well.

Like many perfume videos and other commercials, these ads are now widely available through the website YouTube, which enables fan commentary. YouTube comments are offered in a number of languages, but are generally not especially critical. Instead they tend to follow along the lines of "Best ad ever!," "He's so gorgeous," "I want to be her!," "What is that music?", or in some rare cases, "I want that perfume." Some are more critical, as we shall see later.

Coco Mademoiselle Ads

Chanel's advertisements for Coco Mademoiselle are quite different from the No. 5 ads and clearly reflect the fragrance's younger target audience. Rather than emphasizing luxury in a narrative of female longing, they foreground the independence of a saucy young heroine, most recently portrayed in print and television ads by *Pirates of the Caribbean* actress Keira Knightley.[10] In one of these ads, Knightley bursts in through French windows clad in an over-sized man's white shirt and wearing a bowler hat. Accompanied by saucy music from the classic Nat King Cole song "L.O.V.E." (done here in a cover version by Joss Stone), she tosses aside her shirt and hat. Next she opens her expansive closet and selects a red Lagerfeld-designed Chanel gown to wear. She anoints herself with perfume, also donning a trendy ankle bracelet and elegant chain necklace. Both the bottle and her dress are reflected in multiple mirrors as she embraces a handsome man, throwing back her head to laugh. This Chanel girl is sporty and confident. She subsequently flits like a rare bird in her crimson gown amidst men wearing black tuxedoes at a fancy event. But, notably, in the end, she goes off on her own, prancing down the street, independent and jaunty. One YouTube commenter responds in just the predicted way: "Keira is a perfect choice for Coco Mademoiselle. She's young, fresh, elegant and beautiful in an approachable way. She definitely doesn't have an ice queen look or image." The "ice queen" phrase is clearly an unflattering reference to the more aloof persona of Nicole Kidman in the Chanel No. 5 ads.

Male Perfume Ads

I will now turn, briefly, to make some comparisons between the classic Chanel television ads and some alternatives for male fragrances. There are major differences in style, and it is also interesting to see how such ads track changes in gender roles in the last few decades. Men's prestige fragrance sales are now also very significant, topping $900 million in 2006.[11] But of course, men wearing a scent always run the risk of being regarded as vain or "effeminate." So it is interesting to observe how perfumers and advertising agencies deal with this dilemma.

One way to recognize the extent of anxiety about masculinity aroused by perfume is to look back at some of the best – if also unintentionally funniest – ads for a male fragrance ever produced. These were ads made in Japan in the 1970s for the cologne Mandom starring vigilante hero Charles Bronson.[12] (Apparently it took someone as macho as Bronson to convince men that using perfume or cologne was acceptable.) In one such ad, we watch Bronson driving a sports car to his high-rise office building. Once inside, he sits at a desk wearing his black cowboy hat and stroking his moustache. The narrator intones, "Mandom, the choice of men everywhere, real men with guts, he-men, men of action. It's the real man's cosmetic for real men. Why not try it? Mandom." As if the repetition of the phrase "real men" three times in a row is not quite enough, the film cuts from the urban office to shots of Bronson riding a horse with Monument Valley in the background, slathering on cologne. Other versions of the ad show him sprinkling cologne in rapid alternation with images of him shooting a gun. Obviously, the ad agency would have male viewers believe that Mandom is indeed a cologne for "real men."

Chanel displayed its typical originality and flair in television advertisements for its male fragrance Egoiste. This oddly named fragrance appears to exploit the assumption that women are attracted to narcissistic and indifferent men. In a justly famous sequence from the ad, directed by Jean-Paul Goude, dozens of women opened and closed the shuttered windows of their French balconies in unison, shrieking vituperatively, "Egoiste! Egoiste!" The ad promotes the vision of a perfume that will drive women wild, while simultaneously preserving male privilege and independence.

More recent advertisements for male fragrances have recognized changes in ideals of heterosexual romance while also allowing for the possibility of gay male desire. Most obvious in this group are the numerous Calvin Klein ads, solicitations which have at times run afoul of censors with their overly risqué pedophiliac imagery. Also noteworthy are the androgynous models used to promote Klein's unisex scents such as CKOne. One such advertisement even uses computer technology to "morph" a model's face between sexes in a way that might be either provocative or disturbing to some viewers. Rachel Herz remarks on these ads, with a wit I cannot improve upon, that "the consumers of unisex fragrances are without age, race, or gender. They are blank slates on which desire can be sprayed."[13]

A quite funny German ad for Axe also reflects new gender dynamics. At the start we see a handsome, classically virile man spraying the cologne on himself with wild abandon in an elevator. He departs, whereupon a rather small, wimpy-looking fellow gets on. Soon he is joined by a tall beautiful woman who proceeds to become over-heated enough by the scent left in the elevator to ravage him. She leaves, and we see a picture of him looking dazed and disheveled. In the final sequence, we watch while a male hand clad in a leather glove catches the elevator door. The little man's eyes widen anxiously as a huge biker-type fellow clad in full (gay-signifying) leather regalia begins to eye him salaciously.[14]

A scent that has always coped in an upfront manner with the issue of male fragrance anxiety is Old Spice, advertised as a "manly" scent in ads typically featuring a brawny sailor returning from the sea. While on this topic we cannot neglect to mention the recent brilliant campaign featuring the "man your man could smell like," NFL wide receiver Isaiah Mustafa. The athlete/actor starred in a series of hilarious TV ads for Old Spice during 2010, premiering during a prized expensive Super Bowl timeslot. These ads, accompanied by a massive social network campaign, have now been viewed over 100 million times on YouTube, and they also won an Emmy for their creators. Perhaps more significantly, they boosted sales by 107 per cent, due in part to the intensive social media campaign accompanying them.[15] One key point here is that the ads are explicitly addressed to a female buyer whose sexual desires it purports to elicit and foster. The shirtless Mustafa encourages women to compare him to "their" man and at least acquire a fragrance enabling their man to *smell* like him. Another key point here, of course, is that the audience of women of all races is being courted by a black man. It may not seem surprising in the time of America's first black president to see such a figure also featured in a mainstream ad, but there are still aspects of its racial and sexual dynamics and prejudices that are worth noting. One commentator has even written about "Why the Old Spice Guy is Good for Black America."

> He's everywhere, topless, and smoldering. And not only are his strength, intelligence and beauty at the forefront of his character, they're heralded as being at the apex of manhood. No man, black or white, can ever be as sexy, dynamic, talented and worldly as he, and no woman of any race can or should want to resist him. In day's past, Old Spice Guy would have been seen as threatening, aggressive, certainly unfit for a million-dollar ad campaign. But here in 2010, far from being fearful, America is rushing wildly into his sturdy embrace.[16]

Celebrity Perfumes by Women of Color

I turn now from the Old Spice hero Mustafa to considering perfumes both aimed at and prominently featuring women of color. The perfume market continues to be over-saturated with celebrity fragrances, despite the fact that in recent economic hard times, new entries showed signs of slowing down.[17] Still, the occasional "hit" can re-stimulate interest on the part of cosmetics companies. Some of the very biggest hits have included fragrances fronted by prominent women of color, including Queen Latifah, Beyoncé Knowles, Halle Berry, and Jennifer Lopez. Beyoncé's Heat perfume sells at the mid-range of the marketplace in most major department stores (it is priced from $39–$59). With the advertising giant Coty behind it, it has been a phenomenal success. Like many other current celebrity scents, it is quite sweet and combines fruits and florals with a note described as "almond macaroon." Reaction from reviewers on perfume blogs ranges from "blah" to quite negative. One blogger described it as "canned peaches and unwashed ladyparts. And patchouli. What was I thinking? I had to do a vigorous scrubbing before attacking my falafel."[18] Another, in a more neutral vein, wrote: "I don't find it even slightly sexy, and it isn't what I'd call memorable, but it doesn't much matter: it's by Beyoncé and it isn't a complete mess. People will buy it." The latter point seems indisputable – indeed, the perfume has been hugely successful. It is also easy to find YouTube reviews by young African-American women praising the perfume with claims such as, "It smells really good" and "The bottle is really pretty."

Whether or not a perfume associated with one specific racial or ethnic group is a good thing can be debated. The issues here are somewhat reminiscent of similar ones that have been raised concerning, for example, the black beauty salon as an institution promoting entrepreneurship and independence among black women.[19] *New York Times* perfume columnist Chandler Burr has addressed the issue of what he calls "color coding" in perfume advertising and marketing.[20] There are some clear, well-known distinctions among cultures such as Japan, Europe, and the United States in perfume preferences and associations. The scents that do well in one of these areas often do not in the others. Burr describes in detail how the perfume developer Ronnie Stein did targeted market research on Hispanic women in order to assemble a note with particular appeal to this emerging power in the American buying market. It had to combine a sweet fruity note for Latin *joie de vivre* with sexy and feminine notes (which translated into white florals) and warmth (which required musks).

One could plausibly maintain that the entire perfume industry is still rooted in deep traditions of colonialism and orientalism. (One of the major categories always used in classifying perfumes is "Oriental"). Most perfume fragrances feature particular notes of spices, rare flowers, exotic woods, and resins that are found only in tropical and Eastern regions of the world long associated with European expansionist trade. Even now there are severe restrictions on some of these scent-sources, such as Mysore sandalwood – the trees are protected but still attacked by poachers in southern India. These are the same resources that have prompted wars in the past. Some early perfume advertising for fragrances like Tabu and Jean Patou's Colony are textbook examples of rather shocking racism and colonialism in advertising.[21] Fortunately this point does not pass unnoticed by perfume bloggers. One of them has commented, "In the 1930s, Jean Patou, designer for Josephine Baker, had dedicated Amour Amour, a lilting springlike floral bouquet, to dark-skinned beauties."[22] Since the times when overtly racist ads were acceptable we have switched to more subtle versions, for example, Ralph Lauren's Safari ads featuring well-coifed and remarkably blond adventurers in safari clothes, which were popular during the period when the movie *Out of Africa* was setting style trends. Even today some perfumes trade on surprising forms of near-explicit racism, as with Britney Spears' Blonde Woods or the Banana Republic perfume Alabaster. Again, however, this does not go unnoticed in the blogosphere. One commenter observed, "The problem is that the Alabaster ad circumvents imagination by giving us photos of an overtly sexy, nude, pale, very blond woman who somehow leaves no doubt as to what Alabaster is: white skin and, more broadly, whiteness. This scent celebrates not stone, not sculpture, not sand, but more likely cloistered, fair-skinned maidens and even Southern belles."[23]

Perfume Aesthetics, Erotics, and Ethics

Smell, like the sense of physical taste, tends to be associated with the body, appetite, and desire. Just as the smell of various foods can be enticing or off-putting – prompting salivation or gagging – so can smells of pheromones provide impetus for physical arousal, prompting sexual pursuit or avoidance. Not much has been written in traditional Western aesthetics about the sense of smell. There are, of course, defenders of perfume as a fine art who speak in lofty tones of the art of combining scents and, in particular, of its complexity in this age of created molecules. Perfume resembles other more sensory products such as wine or whiskey where there at least is common recognition of some forms of specialized expertise and rarefied consumption. The "noses" who work for perfume houses strive for harmony and seduction and have remarkable abilities even at the physical level. At the most elite companies the perfumers have achieved such a status that their latest work is anticipated by rabid fans, all accepting as given the artistry of their work. For example, Jean Claude Ellena of Hermès has remarked, "We don't care about celebrities at Hermès, it's the artists who drive us."[24]

As for actual art using scent, there has been some but not a lot of it.[25] Typically, it seems, artists employ *bad* smells in apparent attempts to shock, confronting us with awareness of our own mortality or our bodily processes. I am thinking, say, of Damien Hirst's vitrines with rotting meat and flies, or of Wim Delvoye's massive and complicated machine *Cloaca*, which emulates the digestive processes of the human body. A reviewer commented, "During the exhibition, the smelly assembly line caused quite some consternation. It seemed to bring an infernal message into the world. There is enough dung as it is. Why make more?"[26]

One very intriguing example of collaboration between a perfumer and an art museum involves the Denver Art Museum's commissioning of independent perfumer Dawn Spencer Hurwitz in 2010 to create scents to accompany its *King Tut* exhibit. Following the lead of scientists who have painstakingly reconstructed formulas and traced certain elements in remaining preservatives of Egyptian mummies, Hurwitz re-created several of the kinds of oils, scents, and ointments typically used to prepare the dead for eternity.[27] Reviews indicate that some of these are surprisingly modern in feeling while others display an alien (though still intriguing) sensibility. Many elements of the "ancient" compositions would be quite familiar to contemporary perfumers, such as resins, lilies, spices, and so on.

Perfume is anathema to some feminists because it appears to reinforce views of the female body as a source of degrading natural odors that must be covered over. At the same time, the use of perfume can cast suspicion on a woman as making use of illicit tricks to trap a man: perfume has had associations with dangerous and tempting women dating back at least to Cleopatra. But polemics on perfume being somehow "against" female embodiment can be readily inverted. Elements of some perfumes actually build upon musks or synthetic notes in order to amplify so-called "skanky" aspects of female sexuality. Their goal may be not to cover up allegedly "bad" female odors, but instead to embrace or enhance them. Certain florals such as jasmine and gardenias are in fact praised for their "indolic" (stinky cheese) qualities.

To follow up this point, fragrance can bridge traditional gaps in western thought between the physical and emotional, or the body and the mind. Across diverse cultures, incenses have had a long association with facilitating human meditative states and contact with higher, spiritual realms. Certain fragrances like lavender are now commonly used for aromatherapy and are thought to induce moods of tranquility or peace. In an insightful (though not uncritical) analysis of this idea, titled aptly "The Eros – and Thanatos – of Scents," Richard Stamelman writes,

> In the many images she is given, the scented woman exists in a perpetual state of ambiguity, of decorporealized corporeality: at once a body *and* a soul, a presence *and* an absence. By means of the Eros of scent, woman becomes hybrid, a hyphenated being: visible-invisible, proximate-distant, corporeal-spiritual, ephemeral-enduring, earthly-celestial, base-sublime, primitive-civilized, expressive-mute, innocent-seductive.[28]

A final point in favor of perfume use: we can note how perfume provides links between women across generations. Many women have fond memories of their mothers in terms of particular fragrances, or are reminded of grandmothers and great aunts by a mere hint across a room of the classics Shalimar and Mitsouko. Fragrances can have especially potent significant emotional power in our lives. Rachel Herz describes this in terms of "Proustian memories," which are unusually detailed scent memories.[29] Although these are no more accurate than those elicited by the other senses, there is one significant difference:

> We list more emotions, rate our emotions as having greater intensity, report our memories as being more emotionally laden, and state that we feel more strongly a sense of being back in the original time and place when a scent elicits the past than when that same event is triggered in any other way. I have also found that the amygdale, the wellspring of emotion in our brain, is more highly activated when a person recalls a memory by the scent of a perfume than when a person recalls the same memory as a result of seeing that perfume's bottle, or when he or she sees or smells a nonmeaningful perfume. So scent-evoked memories are different from other types of memory experiences. They are uniquely emotional and evocative – in our minds and in our brains.[30]

Resisting the Fantasy: Erotics and Commodity Fetishism

Many perfume advertisements are so iconic that they have entered into our cultural repertoire. People old enough to remember them will still smile at the lyrics from the notorious Enjoli commercial of the 1970s, where the woman sang proudly, "I can bring home the bacon/fry it up in a pan/And never let you forget you're a man, cause I'm a woman, Enjoli."[31] It would be hard to find an ad for any product that speaks more eloquently about the mixed messages about role expectations in the "Super-woman" era of feminism. In fact, the users of Enjoli might do better by dabbing bacon grease behind their ears, according to critic Tania Sanchez: "The question that women casually shopping for perfume ask more than any other is this: "What scent drives men wild? After years of intense research, we know the definitive answer. It is bacon."[32]

Ultimately, a feminist analysis must ask whether perfume advertisements are morally questionable because of the ways in which they control and manipulate female desire. It is indisputable that they do so, at least to the extent of inspiring purchase – as shown by sales figures in response to particular ad campaigns like the Old Spice ads with Mustafa. However, we need not conclude from this fact alone that consumers are somehow mindless victims of capitalist ideology. But numerous forms of resistance are in evidence. For one thing, many fans of fragrance strongly resist gender stereotypes in attempts to market a scent as *either* male or female. This makes sense, because in reality, given a blind testing situation, it is quite difficult to guess the intended gender of certain perfumes. Prominent perfume blogger Katie Puckrik has described a rather funny experiment showing this as follows:

> A couple of years back, *Allure Magazine* ran a funny "Beauty and the Beat" column where Barneys creative director Simon Doonan did a blind sniff test of celebrity perfumes – and attempted to guess the famous faces behind the juice. Struggling to match a star to what each scent was "saying", Simon attributed Derek Jeter's Driven Black to Rihanna: "very sensitive and girlie". And he was sure that Kanye West was the spokesmodel for Paris Hilton's Fairy Dust: "this is a very fashion-obsessed male with a certain flamboyance."[33]

Another form of resistance to the consumerist ideology of perfume advertisements involves parodies and spoofs. Internet searches readily turn up numerous witty homemade versions of some of the ads I have mentioned. These include parodies of existing ads, such as the Chanel ads featuring Kidman and Knightley, or of Sarah Jessica Parker's perfume ads for Lovely.[34] And there are also clever advertisements for fake perfumes done in the typically overblown style of perfume ads with ridiculous fragrance names. One example advertises a fragrance called Tedium (and we should not forget the Polanski-directed parody for *Greed*). Another hilarious video promotes the cologne Cabbage – pronounced "cah-BAHGE" with a fake French accent. The ad features, among other silly scenes, a man sensuously fondling cabbage leaves and chasing a rolling cabbage as it floats away into the distance.[35]

The Chanel mini-films for No. 5 represent a form of standardized control over female desire through manipulative narratives of romance. This is not surprising, because as many feminists have noted, women respond emotionally to romantic narratives. Writers like Linda Williams, Janice Radway, and Tania Modleski converge in regarding romantic narratives as key to women's erotic arousal.[36] Clearly the Chanel advertisements for No. 5 with their mini-narratives of adventure and romance offer something along these lines. But on the other hand, the ads featuring Keira Knightley for Coco Mademoiselle depict a jauntily independent woman who can take off from her handsome male companions without a second look back, suggesting that things are changing.

As for the elitism of an expensive perfume like those made by Chanel, this too warrants further comment. It is true today of course that Chanel epitomizes norms of French luxury and elite class status. But in fact the life of Gabrielle (Coco) Chanel began in a way that was anything but, as she was born illegitimate and grew up in an orphanage. In addition, she was one of the first successful women in fashion, and her success came precisely because she made clothing that broke ground in designs for the new working woman. The fashion historian Anne Hollander explains:

> Chanel's celebrated inventions clothe a female creature who is all the more sexually interesting for being nobody's doll, besides being nobody's fool. Even further, they suggest an unaggressive physical sensuality, the deep pleasure of a self-contained bodily ease that demands no sacrifice of decorum or starting exotism [sic] to be immediately alluring.[37]

Consumers now display a remarkable level of sophistication about perfume (and other) ads, indicating they are not mere pawns in the hands of mass marketers. Not only does the democratization of opinion in the blogosphere demonstrate this, but also the critical responses that blogs enable. Consider, for instance, that not everyone was sucked in by the romantic, positive narrative of the Jeunet/Tautou ad for Chanel No. 5. Several commentators wrote negatively about the danger of liaisons with complete strangers, whether from STDs or the possibility that your neck-sniffing lover might turn out to be a serial killer like Jean-Baptist Grenouille (the maniac murderer with an overdeveloped sense of smell in Patrick Suskind's 2001 novel *Perfume: The Story of a Murderer*). Commentators also noted the oversimplification and avoidance of pressing modern political issues in staging such an intimate public embrace in the public realm of a train station in a Muslim country. In short, when asked to "share the fantasy," some audience members might do so – but others may categorically refuse.[38]

NOTES

1 For further discussion of smell in relation to the other senses, see Avery Gilbert, *What the Nose Knows: The Science of Scent in Everyday Life* (New York: Crown Publishing, 2008), Cathy Newman, *Perfume: The Art and Science of Scent* (Washington, DC: National Geographic Society, 1998), and Diane Ackerman, *A Natural History of the Senses* (New York: Random House, 1990).

2　See Sarah Mahoney, "High-End Beauty Sales Get Ugly," *Marketing Daily*, March 25, 2009; perfumes account for 32% of the prestige beauty market, http://www.mediapost.com/publications/?fa=Articles.showArticle&art_aid=102876 (accessed August 31, 2009).

3　The video can be seen at http://dazeddigital.com/Fashion/article/1769/1/Francesco_Vezzolis_Greed_Online_Premiere (accessed December 7, 2010).

4　Angela writing on perfume blog *Now Smell This*, August 20, 2007, http://www.nstperfume.com/2007/08/20/chanel-no-5-eau-premiere-fragrance-review/ (accessed April 9, 2011).

5　Luca Turin in Jim Drobnick (ed.), *The Smell Culture Reader* (New York: Berg Publishers, 2006), p. 218.

6　Quoted in Rachel Herz, *The Scent of Desire: Discovering Our Enigmatic Sense of Smell* (New York: Harper Collins, 2007), p. 119.

7　It can be viewed from the Chanel website, http://www.chaneln5.com/en-us/?x=-4&y=-4&width=1288&height=780 (accessed December 7, 2010).

8　The interviews with Jeunet and Tautou appear in the "behind the scenes" section of the Chanel website, http://www.chaneln5.com/en-us/?x=-4&y=-4&width=1288&height=780#/behind-the-scenes (accessed 7 December 7, 2010).

9　Elena Vosnaki in *Perfume Shrine* (blog), http://perfumeshrine.fortunecity.com/blog/entry77.html 06 November 06 (accessed August 31, 2009).

10　http://www.youtube.com/watch?v=5zALNTZ9bNs (accessed December 7, 2010).

11　Herz, *The Scent of* Desire, p. 175.

12　http://www.youtube.com/watch?v=mOWQVd7oFuw&NR=1 (accessed August 31, 2009).

13　Herz, *The Scent of Desire*, p. 313.

14　http://www.youtube.com/watch?v=4c_O2TXWi6g (accessed December 7, 2010).

15　"Old Spice Commercial Increases Sales 107 Percent," July 28, 2010, http://blog.searchenginewatch.com/100728-130002 (accessed December 7, 2010).

16　Tetra Bush, "Why the Old Spice Guy is Good for Black Americans" http://community.livejournal.com/ohnotheydidnt/48925444.html (accessed December 7, 2010).

17　"Eau de Celebrity, Waning, Waning?" *Perfume Shrine* (blog), http://perfumeshrine.blogspot.com/ (accessed September 27, 2009).

18　"Only the Nose Knows For Sure," March 18, 2010, *Perfume Posse* (blog), author identified only as "Nava." http://perfumeposse.com/Full link address is http://perfumeposse.com/2010/03/18/only-the-nose-knows-for-sure/ (accessed April 9, 2011).

19　See Adia M. Harvey, "Becoming Entrepeneurs: Intersections of Race, Class, and Gender at the Black Beauty Salon," in *Race, Class, and Gender: An Anthology*, ed. Margaret L. Andersen and Patricia Hill Collins (Belmont, California: Wadsworth, 7th edn, 2007), pp. 547–557.

20 Chandler Burr, "Color Coded," October 22, 2006.

21 Brian from the blog *I Smell Therefore I Am* http://ismelltherefor eiam.blogspot. com/ explains that Colony was Jean Patou's homage to the French Colonial Expo of 1931. Correct link is http://ismelltherefor eiam.blogspot.com/ search?q=patou+colony (accessed April 9, 2011).

22 Featured Review: Naomi Campbell (plus commentary on perfume and semiotics of race) March 18, NY Fragrance Examiner, Sali Oguri.

23 Carmen Van Kerckhove, "Whiteness in A Bottle: Alabaster Perfume from Banana Republic"; also see Erin Aubry Kaplan, "Banana Republic's New 'Alabaster' Campaign Makes no Bones about Celebrating Whiteness," http:// www.latimes.com/news/opinion/commentary/la-oe-kaplan2jun02,0,1899794. column (accessed April 9, 2011).

24 Quoted in *Perfume Shrine* (blog), http://perfumeshrine.blogspot.com/2006/ 08/essay-on-art-in-perfumery.html (accessed July 7, 2006).

25 See Larry Shiner and Yulia Kriskovets, "The Aesthetics of Smelly Art," *The Journal of Aesthetics and Art Criticism* 65 (2007): 273–286.

26 http://www.artnet.com/magazine/reviews/fiers/fiers1-9-01.asp (accessed December 7, 2010).

27 See Secrets of Egypt collection at the perfumer's website, at https://www. dshperfumes.com/index_pdba.asp (accessed December 7, 2010).

28 Stamelman, "The Eros – and Thanatos – of Scents" in *The Smell Culture Reader,* p. 263, emphasis in the original.

29 Herz, pp. 62–63; some of this is disputed by J. Douglas Porteus in "Smellscape," in *The Smell Culture Reader*, p. 101.

30 Herz, 67–68.

31 http://www.youtube.com/watch?v=4X4MwbVf5OA (accessed April 9, 2011).

32 Tania Sanchez, in Luca Turin and Tania Sanchez, *Perfumes: The Guide* (New York: Viking, 2008), p. 7.

33 http://www.katiepuckriksmells.com/; Review of Thierry Mugler Womanity, *Katie Puckrik Smells* (blog); available on http://www.youtube.com/watch?v= dNTKbnwCAnE&feature=player_embedded (accessed July 28, 2010).

34 http://www.youtube.com/watch?v=HBZty0DfMPU&feature=related (accessed December 7, 2010).

35 http://www.youtube.com/watch?v=PptwgTxPTYc (accessed December 7, 2010). Tedium – male perfume spoof. See also http://www.youtube.com/wat ch?v=MGFvXWDt1RE&feature=related for the Cabbage perfume spoof (accessed December 7, 2010).

36 See Linda Williams, *Hard Core: Power, Pleasure, and the "Frenzy of the Visible"* (Berkeley: University of California, 1999); Janice Radway, *Reading the Romance: Women, Patriarchy, and Popular Literature* (Raleigh: University of North Carolina Press, 1991, 2nd edn); and Tania Modleski, *Loving With a Vengeance: Mass Produced Fantasies for Women*, 2nd edn (New York: Routledge, 2007).

37   Anne Hollander, *Feeding the Eye* (New York: Farrar, Straus and Giroux, 1999), p. 18.

38   I would like to thank Terese Weber for reading an earlier draft and saving me from some embarrassing errors, and the volume's editors for questions that led to substantial revisions and, I hope, improvements.

CHAPTER 6

COMPUTATIONAL COUTURE
From Cyborgs to Supermodels

In the early 1940s Harvard-educated psychologist William Moulton Marston (also known as Charles Moulton) created a woman warrior, an Amazon woman, so powerful that she could single-handedly fight the toughest criminals of her time (which at that point in history happened to be the Nazis). Her strengths came not only from her physical prowess, but also from her fashionable accessories. A golden Lasso of Truth, when wrapped around a thug, could elicit the truth from the fibber despite his best efforts to conceal it. Bulletproof bracelets (combined with the she-warrior's natural agility and flawless aim) kept her intact in the line of fire despite the fact that much of her flesh was exposed. An invisible plane transported her from crime scene to crime scene without threat of detection. And amid all the dodged bullets and punches, throughout all the kicking and fighting, she retained a sex appeal and fashion for the ages. Her daily garb was so memorable that decades later it is still a favorite Halloween costume for those who want to put their inner Amazon on display once a year. This wondrous woman is, of course, Wonder Woman.

Fashion – Philosophy for Everyone: Thinking with Style, First Edition.
Edited by Jessica Wolfendale and Jeanette Kennett.
© 2011 Blackwell Publishing Ltd. Published 2011 by Blackwell Publishing Ltd.

In the world of superheroes clothing has always enhanced physical and cognitive capacities. Batman's cape helps him soar, Spiderman's wrists shoot out multi-functional webs, in The Incredibles the super-heroine Helen Parr (also known as Elastigirl) goes shopping for outfits that fit her unconventional lifestyle: fire-resistant and tear-proof suits (to accommodate her personal super-power: stretching her limbs to improbable lengths). And most recently, Ironman's exoskeleton helps him fly, store solar energy, shoot laser beams, and communicate by radar.

While the runways of Paris and Milan may not quite be ready for designer crime-fighting fashion, the integration of technology and fashion is not so new. Eyeglasses are finely tuned magnifying technology, which graced the pages of *Vogue* through the ages. The cat rimmed glasses of the 1960s made this technology synonymous with iconic sex appeal. The watch – whether it's a pocket watch, leather-banded wristwatch, or a clock face on a ring or a necklace, has also become an indispensable fashionable accessory with technological underpinnings. Even the change in fabrics over time can be seen as part of an evolving integration of fashion and technology. When nylon hit the fashion scene in the form of women's stockings in 1940 it was a monumental change to the silk that was previously used.

We're now entering a generation of wearable technology that goes beyond enhancing our vision and helping us track time. While clothing has traditionally enhanced our appearance (thank you, Wonderbra), and corrected physical imperfections, a new generation of technologically enhanced fashion will change how we use clothing, what we expect of our garments and how we relate to fashion.

Some of the garments currently under development in the unlikely labs of the world's top technical institutions interact with our physical surroundings: solar paneled jackets that store energy, shirts that detect wifi, "invisible" clothing that blends into its surroundings. Other garments are woven not just with cloth and thread, but with micro particles that change the nature of the garment: clothes woven by viruses, shirts with built-in nano-perfume. And still other garments use technology that helps us track our experiences, enhance our memories and enrich our social interactions: garments with built-in recording devices that don't just video our interactions but add layers of semantic tags to the video so that we can revisit, remember, and reflect on our experiences in a way that memory alone does not allow.

What's more, these technologies are being integrated into a form that until now has been reserved for the art world, a form that is as serious about aesthetics as about functionality. Popular culture has already introduced us to the notion of "cyborg," a Terminator-like creature who carries strap-on weapons and computational devices and is commonly portrayed as a grotesque mish-mosh of man and machine. Now we might be looking at a new kind of cyborg, who struts down catwalks in fine fabrics and blinking lights.

In this essay I will show that, much like us, much like our devices, clothing will soon be multi-tasking. Our garments will now *do* things. They will do things with information from the environment, from our bodies, from our social surroundings. They will communicate things about us to others, they will inform us about things we might not otherwise notice.

I will explore several themes. First, portable technology (musical devices, phones, computers) is moving closer and closer to the body, and wearability makes this technology a kind of "second skin." What are the implications of having a second skin that's as high functioning as some of the garments I'll describe? Second, because this new kind of fashion places as much importance on aesthetics as function, the cyborg is then transformed from grotesque to gorgeous. How does this transformation change our relationship to fashion and to technology? Finally, I'll suggest that this attention to aesthetics will integrate these "wearables" into our day-to-day lives so much so that the technology embedded in these garments will serve as a sort of functional extension of self – if not by helping us leap tall buildings in a single bound, then by enriching our memories, helping us express ourselves, and enhancing our interactions with others as well as with the environment. These garments will not only change our relationship with the world of fashion, but will change how we construct the "self." I will explore this idea in the context of the hypothesis of extended cognition, which suggests that cognition does not happen within the confines of the skull, but rather extends to the tools we use out there in the world.

The Fashion

Over the years, we have gone from landlines to cordless phones to cells to Bluetooth devices that tuck into our ears. We've turned desktops to laptops to computers that fit in the palms of our hands and respond to the delicate brush of a finger. Portability is the magic ingredient for any technology of the future.

ADA BRUNSTEIN

But while these devices have become smaller and less conspicuous over time, they are still identifiable as devices that either travel with us or attach onto a part of our bodies. iPods strap onto our arms when we run, headphones duck into our ears, and cell phones strap onto our belts. Wearability offers the ultimate portability. The next step is not only for these devices to become more seamlessly integrated with our garments, but to integrate them in such a way that we are not wired or laden with gear. In fact this step is well under way in the form of wearable fashions, which occupy the space in between handheld devices and bodily implants.[1] These wearable fashions will be our multi-functional "second skin."

The most literal interpretation of "second skin" comes from garments that enhance our physical abilities. In August of 2009 the big controversy in the world of swim competitions was over the swimsuits worn by several world record breakers. The new suits (made from a more rubbery material than before) trap air inside the suit, offering the swimmer a bit more levity in the water. Another example is the idea of a "Gecko Suit"[2] which would enable the wearer to scale up walls in the manner of the ever-impressive gecko. These garments transform our bodies, giving us almost super-human abilities. But wearable technology is reaching far beyond bodily enhancements.

Among the alternating narratives associated with America's iconic superhero, Superman, is the one that says he derives his powers from absorbing the sun's radiation. While our bodies may not be able to make use of the sun's rays in quite the same way, our electronic devices certainly can. Scientists and designers have been working on a wide array of garments that are both wearable and can recharge our cell phones, iPods, and other gadgets. And some of them have been doing it with style. Zegna Sport offers the chic Echotech Solar Jacket, which with 4–5 hours of sunlight can recharge the battery carried within the jacket, as well as activate the heating system inside the jacket's collar.[3] Similarly, the Solar Bikini by Andrew Schneider can recharge your iPod, and the male version (iDrink) can keep your beer cold.[4] All of these products have solar panels built into the garment.

The Compass Coat (designed by Stijn Ossevort) has also taken a device that we would normally carry and built it right into a jacket. The coat helps the wearer find North with illuminated shapes formed by "luminescent wires"[5] embroidered into the fabric. Other garments, like t-shirts that detect wifi and show the signal's strength,[6] perform a function that is normally integrated into a more complicated device.

But not all garments have such pragmatic technological functions. If the first step towards ultimate portability is full integration of the technology and the garments – in other words *easy* wearability – the next step is a serious focus on the aesthetic element, moving us towards *desirable* wearability. How can designers not only make our clothes do the things that portable devices do, but also integrate these new wearables into the realm of fashion – a world defined by craft and form?

Several designers have answered that call, among them, Elena Corchero. Corchero combines the high-tech world of solar energy and with vintage-inspired designs. She creates intricate old-fashioned fans and parasols with solar panels camouflaged within the embroidery. By day the devices function as you might expect – the parasol shields the user from the sun (while absorbing its rays). But by night the parasol becomes a chandelier, using the stored energy to offer a soft glow in a dim room.

Another of Corchero's creations (which she sells in her online boutique, lostvalues.com) also has a double life. The LightGown serves its function as a nightgown, but its aesthetic function is not limited to beautifying the wearer. When the garment is taken off and hung on its charger-hook, it becomes a nightlight framed by the delicate draping pastel silk.[7]

Other designers have taken as their inspiration the reliable staple in every woman's wardrobe – the little black dress. The M-Dress (designed by CuteCircuit) is a black silk dress, which also functions as a cell phone. The wearer inserts a SIM card into a slot under the label so the phone number is the same as her cell phone, and the speaker and microphones are embedded in the sleeve. When the dress-phone rings the wearer answers it simply by moving her hand up to her ear. Moving her hand back down ends the call. The gesture recognition software embedded in the dress allows these natural movements to function as on and off switches.

With this kind of attention to design, we move away from portables and into a world in which glamor itself goes high-tech. And this transition has implications both for how we see ourselves and for how we interact with others. A beautiful dress might make us feel beautiful not only because we encase our bodies in the beauty of that dress but also because of the effect the dress has on its viewers. We construct that beautiful self in our minds in part because of the beholder's reaction. Similarly a black leather jacket covered in zippers might align us with a certain edgy image, created by our perception of the jacket as well as the way in which that jacket interacts with others' fashion sense. If a garment alone can play a role in constructing a *self* both for internal and external examination, what

ADA BRUNSTEIN

happens when that garment does stuff? What role does the additional functionality play in the way we construct ourselves?

Consider our most basic definition of self – embodiment. Throughout various literary explorations of who we are and what we long to be, there have been several recurring themes. We have always longed for the ability to communicate telepathically; we have struggled with the ability to know our own minds and enhance our memory, and, for all of our efforts to leave our individual marks on the world, we have wanted, at times, to be invisible.

In 1897 H. G. Wells published the science fiction novel *The Invisible Man* in which a scientist changes his refractive index to become invisible. In a more modern story, a certain British wizard receives as a gift a magical Cloak of Invisibility, which hides a physical body from the view of most creatures.

In the world of science non-fiction scientists have started to develop the technology that might create such an invisibility cloak. At the moment the material is not quite as effective as those in the novels, (in fact it's not exactly a cloak yet), but it does rely on technology similar to what Wells described in 1897. Two teams led by Xiang Zhang of the Nanoscale Science and Engineering Center at the University of California, Berkeley created artificial materials that bend light backwards as it passes through them. This kind of material has been more than a decade in the making and it does what no natural material can do – it interacts with the magnetic field of light, bending it so an object appears invisible. This is the kind of material that might be used to one day make an invisibility cloak.[8]

While Zhang's research was funded by the government and will likely result in products more for military camouflage than catwalks, Susumu Tachi, an engineer at the University of Tokyo, developed an invisible raincoat that might be more fitting for a fashionista. The technology is a bit of a magic trick. The coat is essentially a movie screen, which takes images captured by a camera on the back of the coat and projects them onto the front so that the front of the coat seems to blend into the background.[9][10]

These products are in their infancy but, given the resources devoted to these efforts, it's not unlikely that they will pave the way for more sophisticated garments, which might eventually come close to their fictional counterparts and allow us to disappear from view. Then what? At the very least our notion of embodied self is linked to the fact that our bodies appear to others as they appear to us.[11] But imagine a runway of the future with a torso that seems to disappear, or an empty space where an arm would normally swing alongside the strut. How might these garments help us play with the notions of bodily beauty?

Consider the variability in the role of exposed skin in the fashion world. Britney Spears's bare midriff was all the rage for a time. Hemlines of the 1960s rose to mid-thigh. In some eras, skin was in. Not so in the 1940s and even Britney is covering her midsection these days. If the degree of skin's exposure is subject to the constraints of the fashion world, why not the degree of exposure of entire limbs? Might visible arms be in one year and "invisible" arms – draped in an invisibility sleeve – in the next? Might an "invisible" midsection be more slimming than black? The very possibility of invisible garments introduces a range of parameters within which to define beauty.

While these wearables (some of which are only glimmers of garments of the future) draw on the environment (the world outside the body) others go entirely the other way and detect information from within the body by monitoring our internal states or reminding us of what's happening in our bodies by analogy. A smoking jacket designed by Fiona Carswell has two plastic lungs placed appropriately on the chest at the front of the jacket. When the wearer smokes, she exhales into a tube that's built into the collar. Over time, if the wearer continues to smoke, the lungs darken.

The LifeShirt, which measures over 30 vital life signs, has more direct medical applications. It has been used in studies to assess the anxiety level in patients with everything from bipolar disorder to breast cancer. The military has also used it to monitor soldiers in training.[12] The shirt is equipped with fabric electrodes and a small unit that the wearer carries in the shirt pocket.

Designer Diana Eng's Heartbeat Hoodie uses a body's internal changes to draw our attention to the external factors that may have caused those changes. In fact, the Hoodie bears some connection to Wonder Woman's Lasso of Truth. William Moulton Marston's lie-detecting lariat wasn't pure science fiction – it had a grain of science truth. Marston's wife once remarked that her blood pressure rose when she got excited. These observations supposedly inspired the systolic blood-pressure test, which Marston invented and which is one of the components of polygraph tests.

Just as Marston's test measures blood pressure, Eng's Heartbeat Hoodie monitors increases in the wearer's heart rate. An algorithm attempts to capture those increases which are more likely to result from excitement than physical exertion, and a camera embedded in the hood takes pictures that coincide with those increases, capturing the presumed source of excitement. Since we're not generally conscious of our heart rate and maybe not always conscious of what causes it to flutter, the pictures are meant to capture those moments of enthusiasm that perhaps fall below the radar by the end of the day. They add a layer of experience that might otherwise have been forgotten.[13]

Much like superheroes' outfits these garments multitask, and these latter garments in particular help reveal layers of our inner selves that we are not otherwise conscious of. While we are constantly interacting with external sources of information (in our overly-wired world), we are not in fact accustomed to interacting with internal sources of information on a day-to-day basis. We know smoking darkens our lungs but we don't normally have a physical reminder – a visual. We can feel the highs and lows of excitement and anxiety, but we don't normally have daily data revealing the details of these states. Garments that monitor those internal states can add layers of self-awareness that in the past were reserved for doctor's offices.

However, among the most intriguing developments in wearables, and the one that may have the most profound implications for our self construction, are the ones that have social functions. The mobile phone dress mentioned above is a striking example. There are no on and off switches. Our movements power the phone on and off, and our bodies become the communication device, mediated by little more than a thin fabric.

The Hug Shirt, which got Time Magazine's nomination for one of the best inventions of 2006, uses internal states to perform a social function. It is essentially a Bluetooth accessory that allows wearers to exchange hugs. Actuators and sensors in the fabric provide the simulated embrace, which is sent from another shirt-wearer who hugs himself to activate the exchange. The sensors deconstruct the hug into pressure, heart rate, and skin temperature, among other things. The cold hard data are then transmitted and, with a little imagination and some intricate technology, those data are reconstructed in the other shirt and experienced as a hug by the wearer.[14]

A few other examples show the range of communicative activities that designers are building into our day-to-day garments. The Skirteleon (by CuteCircuit) changes colors and patterns depending on the mood and activity of the wearer, measured through touch sensors.[15] Barking Mad, (by Suzi Webster) is a coat for the shy fashionista. It senses when others infringe on the wearer's personal space and lets out a bark through the speakers inside the coat.[16] A jumpsuit called <random> search records the activity surrounding a body search in contexts such as airports or other high security areas.[17] The designer Ayah Bdeir created the suit in defense of those who are illegally searched or violated during a random search. She calls them search "victims."

Jacket Antics, designed by Barbara Layne, display LED texts and designs on the back of the jackets the way a t-shirt might display a slogan or a wisecrack. But this jacket has two differences. One is that the messages move and change. The other is that when two people wearing the jacket hold hands, the displays sync up so that the words run across in a continuous message from one jacket to the next. Since the wearers don't see the messages (because they appear on their backs), the real effect is to convey a sense of togetherness to others (reinforcing the handholding, which, of course, also conveys togetherness).[18]

Some garments are meant to capture and perhaps add layers of meaning to our daily experiences. Designer Diana Eng (Heartbeat Hoodie designer) first hit the national scene as a contestant on the second season of Bravo's hit show Project Runway. Her mathematically inspired designs got her through six episodes of the show. Shortly afterwards her design Blogging In Motion won Yahoo Hack Day 06 ("Project Runway for computer nerds"). Blogging In Motion is simply a handbag combined with a pedometer and a camera. Every few paces a cell phone camera snaps a picture, sends the image to Flickr and uploads it onto a blog.[19] While for most of us pictures of every 30 paces of our day would hardly be exciting, it's not that far a cry from Facebook's status updates, which have helped glorify the mundane.

My personal favorite of the socially inspired garments is Intimate Controllers. These are two-piece bra and bottoms for a woman, and shorts for a man, each with sensors strategically placed throughout the garments, which the other person controls. The garments are essentially joysticks for a video game the couple plays. As they increase the level of the game, they are prompted to use the sensors placed closer to the more sensitive areas of the wearer – the shoulder controls might be used at level one of the game, but by level three the man must reach close to the woman's cleavage to play.[20]

Finally, Elena Corchero (who designed the vintage-inspired garments and has emerged as my favorite designer of wearable technology) along with Stefan Agamanolis developed a garment that is wearable poetry as much as wearable technology. The whiSpiral is a luxurious white synthetic fur wrap equipped with nine hidden mini-recorders, each of which record up to 10 seconds' worth of messages from friends. When the wearer wraps the garment around her shoulders, or when she caresses one of the sensors, the pre-recorded voices speak, creating a sense of connection and intimacy even in solitude.[21]

These garments, some of which appeared at the SIGGRAPH 2007 show called UnRavel, expand the range of the wearer's interaction with the world. As UnRavel curator Amanda Parkes put it, because clothing is "a second skin" and technology is so ubiquitous, technologically based garments become a "natural interface with the world."[22] But if it becomes "natural" for that interface to be on us for most of our waking hours, how will this development shape who we are and how we think?

Cyborgs and Supermodels

Some have described Professor Steve Mann as the first cyborg. Mann, who has been creating wearable technology for two decades, is depicted in photographs over the years wearing bulky head gadgets with antennae reaching skyward, among other strapped-on machines.[23] The head gadget, a pre-cursor to WearCam, was meant to be a wearable computer equipped with cameras, microphones, speakers and display capabilities.[24]

Today's wearable technology bears little resemblance to Mann's cyborg or the fictional cyborgs that look half man and very much half machine. But there is a common thread, so to speak. The garments in both cases enhance the wearer's abilities. The difference, however, is fashion. In fact Mann himself has since upgraded the WearCam to look more like a sleek pair of sunglasses. No antennae are required. Because designers are weaving technology into the fabrics they work with, cyborgs may soon look more like supermodels, draped in grace, elegance, and *cool*. Where man and machine were once separate, they are now moving towards integration. Where the form of fashion and function of technology were in many ways separate, we are now moving towards integration. The *cyborg* is going glam.

One way to look at this integration between fashion and technology is simply to note that we've long been making technology as portable as possible, and as mentioned above, wearability provides the ultimate portability. We could simply say that integrating technology into clothing is part of this trend and the fact that there's an integration of design (fashion) and technology is not notable given that aesthetics have long been a part of design schemes for most technologies (cars, refrigerators, cell phones, corkscrews, and so on).

On the other hand it's worth exploring what happens when devices that enhance our interaction with the world get so close to our bodies. How might the garments described above change how we behave with respect to others and how we think of and experience "self?" A friend once searched his house for his eyeglasses, while wearing those very glasses. I turned my house upside down searching for my cell phone ... while talking on that very phone. This never happened on my tethered landline. This sort of thing happens when technology is not *with* us but *on* us ... when the physical act of porting a device, and the physical constraints of a wired or tethered device disappear. When the intermediate steps between our mental acts (talking) and physical acts (moving towards the phone, picking it up, dialing) diminish, the technology that makes that possible becomes an extension of us – a physical appendage with social/cognitive functions.

In "A Cyborg Manifesto"[25] University of California Santa Cruz professor Donna Haraway defines cyborg as "a cybernetic organism, a hybrid of machine and organism, a creature of social reality as well as a creature of fiction." She goes on to describe how cyborg imagery can help us change our notion of self. *Wired* magazine's Hari Kunzru summarized the dense text perfectly:

> In the manifesto, Haraway argues that the cyborg – a fusion of animal and machine – trashes the big oppositions between nature and culture, self and world that run through so much of our thought. Why is this important? In conversation, when people describe something as natural, they're saying that it's just how the world is; we can't change it.
>
> Women for generations were told that they were "naturally" weak, submissive, overemotional, and incapable of abstract thought. That it was "in their nature" to be mothers rather than corporate raiders, to prefer parlor games to particle physics. If all these things are natural, they're unchangeable. End of story. Return to the kitchen. Do not pass Go. On the other hand, if women (and men) aren't natural but are constructed, like a cyborg, then, given the right tools, we can all be reconstructed.[26]

The context of Haraway's Manifesto is broad social politics, but her ideas can also frame a discussion of personal interactions and relationship to self.

Haraway's notion of cyborg is not the grotesque man-machine. Her cyborg is a creature embedded in networks. As she told *Wired*, "Human beings are always already immersed in the world, in producing what it means to be human in relationships with each other and with objects." ... "If you start talking to people about how they cook their dinner or what kind of language they use to describe trouble in a marriage, you're very likely to get notions of tape loops, communication breakdown, noise and signal – amazing stuff." Kunzru aptly observes that "even while we mistake ourselves for humans, the way we talk shows that we know we're really cyborgs."[27]

Taking this view, wearable technology is just one more example of a tool for functioning within a network. We are already communicative creatures. We're now developing tools to expand that communication in such a way that we don't have to reach for *other* devices. Instead the functionality becomes part of a reconstructed *self*.

But what exactly is the nature of that reconstructed self if our clothed bodies become the tools? Philosophers and cognitive scientists have long been exploring the nature of cognition. What does it mean to know? To think? And where do we look for the answer to those questions? Do we look to the brain and say that whatever mechanisms we use for thought live within the confines of our skull? Does the mind come equipped with all the tools it needs for cognition and does it simply rely on those tools in order to make sense of the external world? Or is there an alternative?

In an essay called "The Extended Mind," Andy Clark and David Chalmers propose a concept they call "active externalism." They suggest that our cognitive processes – the way we process, experience and know the world – do not occur solely within our epidermal cloak. The tools we use, the objects we interact with, actually assist and help shape our thinking.[28] They cite a study that uses the video game Tetris as an example.

> In Tetris, falling geometric shapes must be rapidly directed into an appropriate slot in an emerging structure. A rotation button can be used. David Kirsh and Paul Maglio (1994) calculate that the physical rotation of a shape through 90 degrees takes about 100 milliseconds, plus about 200 milliseconds to select the button. To achieve the same result by mental rotation takes about 1,000 milliseconds. Kirsh and Maglio go on to present compelling evidence that physical rotation is used not just to position a shape ready to fit a slot, but often to help determine whether the shape and the slot are compatible. The latter use constitutes a case of what Kirsh and Maglio call an "epistemic action." Epistemic actions alter the world so as to aid and augment cognitive processes such as recognition and search. Merely pragmatic actions, by contrast, alter the world because some physical change is desirable for its own sake (e.g., putting cement into a hole in a dam).[29]

Active externalism, according to Clark and Chalmers, refers to the role that the environment plays in "driving cognitive processes."[30] How might we view wearable technology through this lens? Consider these different ways of placing a phone call:

1   Walking to a landline phone, removing the phone from its cradle, pushing buttons corresponding to a phone number (or placing a finger in a hole corresponding to a number and then rotating the wheel of holes once for each number), hanging up to end the call.
2   Taking a cell phone out of a pocket or handbag in the middle of the sidewalk, clicking a button, speaking the name of the person you want to reach, clicking a button to end the call.
3   Clicking a button on a Bluetooth, speaking the name of the person you want to reach, clicking a button to end the call.
4   Raising your hand to your ear, speaking a name, lowering your hand to end the call.

Our understanding of what it means to call someone is drastically different from the first option to the fourth. In option four, our bodies – our arms in particular – can serve as proxies to place calls. This is a profound shift from placing a call using a device that we manipulate.

Now imagine entire outfits that perform computational and communicative tasks. If active externalism is a real possibility, if we can indeed alter our thinking through the tools we use, then our garments' functionality will become a part of our thought process. They will become a part of a *self* which can talk to absent interlocutors, express our moods non-verbally (not necessarily even consciously), embrace remotely, and track the momentous events in our day, all without interacting with a device – all through little more than the clothes on our backs.

And just as a pair of glasses can feel so much a part of a face that the wearer forgets his vision isn't quite as good as that, and just as I can talk into a device and forget there's a device there at all, we may, perhaps, experience similar momentary lapses in our understanding of where we end and our wearable technology begins. Our garments' functionality may become so much a part of the reconstructed self – so much an expansion of how we understand our interaction with the world – that we might at some point raise our bare arm to an ear expecting to answer a call, unaware that we are not wearing the garment that would make that possible. Or we might squeeze our naked arms only to find that the skin hangs impotent on our bones, unable to give or receive an embrace because we're not wearing the right shirt. We might wonder if, at some point in the future, the naked body would ever feel adequate again.

Wearable technologies have implications for our personal interactions and for our behavior within society as well. The Hug Shirt, for example, raises interesting questions about physical privacy. What if the person whose hug you welcome today becomes the person whose touch you can't stand tomorrow? What measures can the designers implement to prevent unwanted "hugs"?

And out on city streets life is already different with the ubiquity of mobile devices. Consider that only a decade ago we might have steered clear of the man on the street who was muttering to himself. Now people frequently roam the streets engaged in lively conversation with no visible interlocutor. Now, we just assume there is a Bluetooth or other device hidden behind the ear by a head of hair.

Saying "excuse me" or even honking a horn doesn't always have the effect it used to. The ear we want to bend is oftentimes rapped with attention to the tunes emanating from barely visible devices. Wearables already have us behaving differently and expecting different behaviors from others.

The transition to this kind of fashion – this kind of technology – will be thrilling to watch. And the integration of beauty, style and desirable wearability with the functionality of what have become our most necessary tools, will be a welcome change. But it should be a change that prompts much thought and consideration about who we will become.

In a sense, the integration of fashion and technology – the new, stylish cyborg – is a self-fulfilling prophecy. The superheroes we created may not have come from pure fantasy. Perhaps they came from a long-standing need to be more than we are. Maybe we created the characters we always wanted to become and we need only look at those creations to see a glimpse of our future selves.

NOTES

1 Sabine Seymour, *Fashionable Technology*, (Springer 2008), 14.
2 http://www.darpa.mil/dso/thrusts/materials/biomat/zman/index.htm (accessed November 23, 2010).
3 http://www.treehugger.com/files/2009/10/finally-attractive-solor-clothing-the-zenga-ecotech-solar-jacket.php (accessed November 23, 2010).
4 http://andrewjs.com/solarbikini.html (accessed November 23, 2010).
5 Seymour, *Fashionable Technology*, p. 71.

6   http://www.thinkgeek.com/tshirts/illuminated/991e/ (accessed November 23, 2010).

7   http://www.lostvalues.com (accessed November, 23 2010).

8   http://www.reuters.com/article/idUSN1029418920080810?pageNumber=1 &virtualBrandChannel=0 and http://www.technologyreview.com/Nanotech/ 21213/?a=f (accessed November 23, 2010).

9   http://www.wired.com/wired/archive/11.08/pwr_invisible.html (accessed November 23, 2010).

10 A video of "invisible" objects and the invisible raincoat: http://www.youtube. com/watch?v=zDbnqc26CyQ (accessed November 23, 2010).

11 Barring disorders that skew body image.

12 http://www.pdacortex.com/VivoMetrics_FDA.htm (accessed November 23, 2010).

13 http://www.trendhunter.com/trends/heartbeat-hoodie-by-diana-eng (accessed November 23, 2010).

14 http://www.cutecircuit.com (accessed November 23, 2010).

15 Seymour, *Fashionable Technology*, p. 42.

16 Seymour, *Fashionable Technology*, p. 63.

17 Seymour, *Fashionable Technology*, p. 150.

18 http://www.youtube.com/watch?v=B9obd_JRgek (accessed November 23, 2010).

19 http://techcrunch.com/2006/10/01/all-women-team-takes-yahoo-hack-day-top-prize/ (accessed November 23, 2010).

20 http://jennylc.com/intimate_controllers/ (accessed November 23, 2010).

21 http://web.media.mit.edu/~stefan/hc/projects/whispiral/ (accessed November 23, 2010).

22 http://www.youtube.com/watch?v=j5SoPlVajsA (accessed November 23, 2010).

23 http://wearcam.org/pictures.html (accessed November 23, 2010).

24 http://n1nlf-1.eecg.toronto.edu/personaltechnologies/ (accessed November 23, 2010).

25 Donna Haraway, "A Cyborg Manifesto: Science, Technology, and Socialist-Feminism in the Late Twentieth Century," in *Simians, Cyborgs and Women: The Reinvention of Nature* (New York; Routledge, 1991), pp. 149–181.

26 http://www.wired.com/wired/archive/5.02/ffharaway_pr.html (accessed November 23, 2010).

27 http://www.wired.com/wired/archive/5.02/ffharaway_pr.html (accessed November 23, 2010).

28 Clark and Chalmers, "The Extended Mind," *Analysis* 58 (1998): 7–19.

29 Clark and Chalmers, "The Extended Mind."

30 Clark and Chalmers, "The Extended Mind."

PART 3

FASHION, IDENTITY, AND FREEDOM

CHAPTER 7

WEARING YOUR VALUES ON YOUR SLEEVE

At the Summer Olympics in 1968, two Americans, Tommie Smith and John Carlos, won the gold and bronze medals respectively in the 200-meter race. At the awards podium during the medal ceremony, Smith wore a black scarf, both were shoeless and wearing only black socks, and both raised black-gloved hands in an iconic moment that memorialized their solidarity with an oppressed community.

I have always been fascinated by the way that ordinary, simple things like a scarf and two black gloves can trigger in our minds a nexus of significant, complex issues involving justice, autonomy, and moral solidarity. Things like scarves and gloves can do this because there is a connection between the *obviously* profound issues of autonomy and moral solidarity on the one hand and the *seemingly* trivial subject of wardrobe style on the other. One of the primary ways we navigate our relationships with other persons, competing values, and even with ourselves is by means of social practices involving the adornment of our bodies. Of course, it is not *just* with clothing that we do this. There are other social practices that represent our shared fascination with autonomy and moral solidarity,

Fashion – Philosophy for Everyone: Thinking with Style, First Edition.
Edited by Jessica Wolfendale and Jeanette Kennett.
© 2011 Blackwell Publishing Ltd. Published 2011 by Blackwell Publishing Ltd.

but one of the most visible and ubiquitous has to do with a daily necessity: dressing ourselves!

I admit that it may sound initially odd to claim that clothing has become a focal point for articulations of autonomy and moral solidarity. In the remainder of this brief exploration, I want to highlight some of these connections. While my main emphasis is on *moral solidarity*, I need to set up that discussion by first saying a few things about *autonomy* and *authenticity*. These three things are close to the heart of what it means to have a high quality of human life. Insofar as garments have become embedded within these deeply human values, this makes a concern about style, despite some of its excesses and silliness, philosophically interesting because human beings are philosophically interesting.

What makes for a good quality of life? Philosophers have given many answers that differ greatly in the details, and this is understandable. After all, the world is populated by very different personalities, and a boring world it would be if we were all too similar. Do the different answers nevertheless share a theme? One familiar thread cites autonomy as central to a good quality of life. It is extraordinarily difficult to say exactly what autonomy is, but for our purposes a sketch will suffice. It has something to do with having the freedom to guide our lives by our own beliefs, desires, and goals. Our level of autonomy directly affects things like our career choices, how we conduct ourselves in relationships with other persons, how we vote during election seasons (and, depending on our political system, whether we get to vote at all), how we spend our money, what organizations with which we align ourselves, and so on. Our desires, beliefs, and goals – things that we might say are *internal* to us – touch upon everything that is *external* to us. How we evaluate our lives surely incorporates both the internal and external dynamics of our agency. There is thus a vested interest in ensuring that the desires, beliefs, and goals and the choices based on them are authentically our own rather than products of someone else's compulsion. In a nutshell, that's a large part of autonomy, and we can see why it's so vital to the goodness of our lives.

How is this related to a concern about clothing style? In the United States, one example of the connection is represented by the controversies over policies concerning public school uniforms. On one side are advocates of compulsory school uniforms who cite their correlation with higher test scores and other positive educational outcomes (for example, higher attendance rates, lower levels of gang involvement, decrease in on-campus violence, and so on). On the other side are critics who argue

DANIEL YIM

that the ability of students to express themselves by means of their outfit choices is a crucial part of their dignity and development as persons.[1] Not only do some critics question the nature of the correlation between uniforms and education outcomes, but they argue that *even if* the correlations were present, that still would *not* justify compulsory uniform codes. These controversies have regularly appeared for litigation in the US Supreme Court.[2] An early prominent example was *Tinker v. Des Moines School District* (1969) where the court established a Constitutional right to self-expression for public school students. It is quite fascinating that the legal arguments have centered around issues of the First Amendment and concerns about individual autonomy versus institutional abuse of power.

Without the connection between how much we value autonomous self-expression and its articulation in clothing style, there would be no argument with the advocates of compulsory school uniforms. Without that connection, the controversy would appear silly and may nevertheless appear so to those who are less familiar with the American scene. The argument about school uniforms is *not* about *whether* there is a connection between clothing style and autonomy. Both sides would agree that there is some connection. The argument is about *how much* to weigh this connection in settling the dispute.

Another example of the relation between fashion and autonomy is found in a clothing line ironically and subversively labeled "Fashion Freaks." The line is the brainchild of Swedish entrepreneur and activist Susanne Berg and Australian textiles specialist Meagan Whellans.[3] They received some grant money from the General Heritage Fund of Sweden to support a line of garment patterns for persons who use wheelchairs. These patterns may be obtained free of charge by persons who use wheelchairs, providing them the liberty to create and modify their distinctive sensibilities of style beyond the constricted options currently available. Berg humorously states the obvious when she says, "It's not always fun to go to a pub in comfy jogging pants – it doesn't fit with your identity and is not going to help you pick someone up!" Underneath the humor is a rather serious point. How we dress is fundamentally an extension of our dignity, because the adornments of our bodies are an expression of our autonomy and uniqueness. They are an extension of our presence or in Berg's word, "identity." The contemporary French philosopher Hélène Cixous writes of the famous fashion designer and writer Sonia Rykiel, "The dress by Sonia Rykiel doesn't surprise me. It comes to me, agrees with me, and me with it, and we resemble one another. Between us is the memory of a nomadic fire. The dress dresses a woman I have never known and who is also me."[4]

Cixous is poetically expressing how clothing should be understood fundamentally as an extension of one's body and presence, not merely a covering. If this is true, then the kinds of limitations faced by persons who use wheelchairs on ranges of choice for something as *seemingly* trivial as a wardrobe can be experienced as a limitation on one's ability to actualize one's autonomy. This is what makes something like Fashion Freaks newsworthy. The high demand for their clothing patterns is evidence that control of how one adorns one's body connects deeply with autonomous self-expression, which itself is part of the good life.

I've so far only mentioned the power of choice. There is more, however, to autonomy. It is not enough that the desires, beliefs, goals, and actions be our own. They have to be authentic. Authenticity is a slippery notion. Perhaps an analogy from another domain will help. I am embarrassed to admit how much I love *Antiques Road Show*, an American PBS series about regular people bringing sundry items such as family heirlooms and discarded stuff found in their attics for appraisal by expert antique dealers. These antiquarians uncover the history of these items and help the owners assess the authenticity of their family legends concerning the items in question. In that context, authenticity refers to the degree of fit between the legends and the items' actual histories. In some cases, there is a delightful (and sometimes very profitable) match, and in others, giant bubbles are burst. The magic of the show lies in the examination and testing of the provenance of these items.

It is the notion of testing that is crucial, and its importance carries over quite well to authenticity in the domain of beliefs, desires, and goals. John Stuart Mill, an English philosopher and social reformer of the eighteenth century, was in many ways far ahead of his time. In his famous essay *On Liberty*, Mill argued that society would gradually improve if individuals were given the social and legal freedom to express their beliefs not just in words but also in what he called "experiments in living." This phrase simply refers to putting into practice one's values and desires in the choices one makes about things such as career, relationships, course of education, and communal associations. The point of experiments in living is three-fold. First, Mill takes freedom of thought and the corresponding freedom of expression in lifestyle as two inseparable sides of a coin. Second, when all individuals are expressing themselves in this free manner, there is ample opportunity for one to encounter beliefs, desires, and lifestyles very different from one's own. Third and related to

DANIEL YIM

the second, these various experiments in living offer a marketplace of ideas and lifestyles that serves as a test for whether or not one really holds to one's *professed* beliefs, desires, and alleged choices. While Mill's vision is a bit idealistic, his core point makes sense. How would you know whether or not you truly believe something unless you experienced an alternative and had the chance to compare your beliefs with the alternative? Isn't this why we value education (as opposed to indoctrination)? Ideally, education frees us to examine our beliefs against a wide range of evidence and experience. Only then can we say that we are approaching a level of authenticity in our autonomy.

The importance of this was sharply illustrated to me recently as I was in a clothing store. (This example may appear trite, but it does so only to those of us who have forgotten our pre-teen years when these experiences mattered quite a bit.) As I write this essay, it is close to the end of summer in the United States, and this portends great change to the weathered eye of public school students everywhere. It's time for back-to-school shopping. Inside the store in question, I witnessed an intense discussion between a mother and daughter about clothing choices. The mother was "encouraging" her daughter to retain a style of dress that maintained what must have been a family history of *very* modest clothing, style, and sensibility (for example, ankle-length dresses, full-length jumpers, and so on). The daughter was tentatively but consistently asserting her preference for attire that was a bit more expressive, such as knee-length skirts and tank tops with thicker shoulder straps (still I suspect to most of us safely within the realm of modesty).

Essentially, I was witnessing a young moral agent starting to experiment with a different path than the one followed by her family. While the specific issue was focused on fashion, the deeper issue of the moment concerned rival values having to do with modesty and self-presentation. The mother clearly wanted her daughter not only to dress conservatively but also to *be* conservative in her stances across a wide range of issues. Their conversation turned to things having to do with boys, dating, going to parties, and other precarious subjects, and the mother was predictably conservative about all of these bugbears.

Their initial disagreement about choices in bodily presentation formed a hub that connected naturally to all these other touchy subjects. The daughter was in the process of testing whether the stances she inherited from her upbringing were authentic *for her*, and one of the ways she was testing her commitment was through clothing. Her experimentation signified a deeper moral conversation that the daughter was having with her mother but more importantly with herself, and this is precisely why this particular mother was alarmed. This whole scene is at once mundane and profound because of the entanglement of autonomy with the already value-laden phenomena of clothing and self-presentation.

The investigation has thus far been focused on the individual, and appropriately so since the individual is the root of autonomy. Most of us, however, live in a world of associations with communities of persons with whom we possess varying degrees of solidarity. In fact, very few of us actually live the caricature of the "rugged individualist." Our autonomy is expressed in the form and content of our social engagement, almost *never* in detachment. Marilyn Friedman, a contemporary American philosopher, has written about the need to revise the notion of autonomy so that we understand it as moving authentically *towards* social engagements of loyalty and commitment. In other words, autonomy involves directing ourselves into relationships and communal solidarity based on values that we authentically choose for ourselves.[5] Alexis de Tocqueville, a French political historian, traveled through America in the early 1800s and wrote a classic work of political science titled *Democracy in America*. In that massive tome, he ruminates on the way that liberty in America is expressed through the voluntary associations into which citizens enter. From his perspective, these associations are natural expressions of liberty and the desire to choose one's peers, but they also serve a greater purpose: that of the individual rising above narrow self-interest into communal solidarity. The kinds of associations that Tocqueville had in mind are the ones that have lasting power in nearly every human society, including the most visible and controversial ones clustered around religion and politics.

Why are these associations so important? I cannot give a full explanation, since I'm no psychologist, but I can speak from common experience. Not only is this behavior part of our evolutionary heritage, but it is also immensely enjoyable. Consider how fulfilling it is to meet others who are like-minded. It is enjoyable and satisfying to be in relationships with other persons who share one's values, see the world in similar ways, interpret reality in ways consistent with one's own perspective, and acknowledge the value and legitimacy of one's way of negotiating a private and public life. That's solidarity in a nutshell. Maybe that's what we mean when we say approvingly of someone or a group that we "speak the same language."

I do not mean to suggest the cartoonish view of solidarity in which everyone is a clone of the other. Even in very ideologically centered groups, there are important differences between individuals. Nevertheless, the differences in these tightly centered groups are typically of two types. They could be differences about how to articulate a core value. For example, I have friends who are committed locavores,[6] but they have disagreements about the role that farmers' markets actually play in the locavore ethic. They do not disagree about the core importance of eating local, sustainable foods, but they disagree about how best to put into practice their shared food ethic. The other type of difference could be about issues that are important but tangentially related to some core values. For example, these same friends also disagree about the criteria for "organic food." This is an important issue, but it is somewhat tangential. Admittedly I'm working with some idealized types of moral solidarity. Rarely is the soul of a group so consistent, but working within a framework of idealized types makes it a little easier to think through the ways that autonomy, authenticity, and solidarity intersect with bodily adornment.

That said, how one dresses can communicate one's associations and values. There are tragic cases where this phenomenon ends with ruin. Consider the case of triple murder in San Francisco in June of 2008.[7] Forty-eight-year old Anthony Bologna, and his two sons Michael and Matthew, aged 20 and 16 respectively, were shot to death in their family car. It was a case of mistaken identity. Members of the MS-13 gang mistook them as rivals due to their fashion sensibilities involving baseball caps, hairstyles, and colors. About one year later in the same city involving the same gang, another case of mistaken identity claimed the life of 21-year-old college student Moises Frias, Jr, again for the very same reasons.[8]

What makes these tragedies of violence possible is not clothing *per se* but rather the manner in which its presentation is already wrapped up with communal solidarity, whether it be in religious groups, political associations, cultural groups, or gangs. I would like to explore several examples to illustrate the connection. The examples will be drawn from modern and contemporary cases to showcase the manner in which fashion is deeply implicated in moral solidarity.

Allow me to transition to an anecdote far removed from the heavy seriousness of gang violence. About two years ago, I was at a party populated by a crowd of 20- and 30-somethings. The partiers were extremely trendy and image conscious. Photographers from *Esquire* magazine were asking attendees to fill out waivers so that the magazine could use shots of the crowd. It was that sort of scene. There was one young woman present who wore a shirt bearing the motto, "Fashion is slavery!" Presumably the message is that being a person who is fashion conscious is somehow a defect of character. The irony of the situation was that this young woman was carefully dressed as a near cartoon of "anti-establishmentarian" garb. She wore Doc Marten boots with big soles, purposefully overwrought horn-rimmed eyeglasses, a black and red checkered miniskirt designed to be a clashing mix of a traditional pattern with scandalous length, and so on. I was certain that she was being purposefully ironic about the whole scene. She had to be playing a sophisticated joke on everyone by combining outmoded anti-establishmentarian motifs at this particular party. I discovered that in fact she intended no irony. She was totally serious … and utterly blind to her own meticulous "slavery" to fashion. She thought she had risen above fashion, but she managed only to be in the grip of an alternative fashion closely guided by an even more specific cluster of values. In fact, this young woman was actually doubly conscious. She needed to display a constant awareness of prevailing fashions in the community she critiqued and to adjust her own responses along the calculated lines of her code of protest.

This shows that it is extraordinarily hard to be anti-fashion in any kind of self-conscious, value-driven way. It might even be impossible, since in proclaiming oneself to be anti-fashion for moral or political reasons, one is forced by necessity to select an alternative.

I learned of a less ironic (and more coherent) example of solidarity through protest several years ago while working at a hotel to help pay my way through college. One of my coworkers was from Israel, and she lived for a time in a Kibbutz. I had no idea what that meant, and she explained to me a little bit of the history of the Kibbutz movement in modern Israel. The early Kibbutz was a uniquely Israeli community phenomenon. It was a village where communitarian living was the rule. It began early in the twentieth century and evolved into a distinctive part of Israeli culture by the 1940s. The movement has largely declined, but there are still a few faithful practitioners and outposts. It was originally based upon a fusion of Marxist and Zionist principles about shared means of production and the equitable allocation of resources among members of this voluntary community.

Early in the Kibbutz movement, one of their distinctive ways of expressing their values and displaying their solidarity had to do with clothing.[9] Women and men wore very plain garments and shoes for both work and leisure. Women wore a Ukrainian style jumper dress called the

DANIEL YIM

sarafin, and men wore simple Russian shirts and straw hats. In the early stages of this movement, clothing from person to person was similar if not identical, even approaching androgynous emphasis of function over style. The plain construction (for example, designed for labor, muted natural colors, and so on), combined with the conspicuous lack of accessorizing, communicated their moral point of view regarding material simplicity, and in the case of women's clothing, chastity and modesty.

These choices allowed them to articulate their moral stances in the mode of solidarity, but there is also the flip side of like-mindedness. How the body is presented in clothing offers a context for disagreement and inter-community critique. In the Kibbutz, the values of material simplicity and modesty were polarized *against* what was perceived by members of that community as dangerous excesses of Western materialism, individualism, and the assault on traditional moral values. These communal stances *pro* and *contra* were strongly expressed through intentional decisions about clothing.

A modern American articulation of this is found in the Amish religious communities. In general, their clothing is made of plain, dark fabrics. Men typically wear simple trousers without crease or cuff, suspenders (belts are not allowed), and plain coats (lapels are discouraged). There are rules about when men may have facial hair and of what type. For example, mustaches are never allowed, and beards are allowed only after a man is married. Women typically wear ankle length dresses that are almost always covered with an apron. Jewelry or other types of accessories are strictly forbidden. Their hair may never be cut but must also be covered by a suitable "head covering" such as a bonnet. Their garb embodies their interpretation of humility and simplicity. The restriction concerning hair is a way of coding very specific and traditional norms about gender roles that are deemed "natural." Overall, their message is one of separation from the outside world, and this separation consists in strong judgments *against* the values and possibilities that shape communities outside their own.[10]

Communities such as the early Kibbutz and Amish offer very distinctive forms of moral solidarity visibly communicated through the way they dress their bodies. In this respect clothing can create, shape, and maintain lines of solidarity through its iconographic nature. There is always the danger of the darker side. This can be deployed to enforce and indoctrinate the members of a community. This happens in much less formal ways as reported in the *Wall Street Journal*.[11] Pre-teens at a Canadian public school regularly experience ridicule for fashion choices having to do with something as simple as colors. That is not quite the kind of indoctrination that elicits the greatest worries. Larger worries have to do with the more severe articulations of social coding through clothing, perhaps precisely in contexts such as the Amish experience.

Earlier in this essay, I talked a bit about authenticity and the virtue of being able to experience different kinds of values in order to test one's own convictions. In the Amish community, there is something like that process. It is called Rumspringa ("running around"), and it was immortalized in the absolutely fascinating, aptly named documentary *The Devil's Playground*.[12] This series, which felt like a splendid hybrid between documentary and reality TV, followed the escapades of a few Amish teenagers who engaged in Rumspringa, a ritual during which Amish teens leave their communities to live outside the confines of the customary rules that govern Amish life. After this process during which they are allowed to experiment with alcohol, drugs, and premarital sex – customs that the Amish refer to as "English" – they are given a choice to return to the fold. The idea is that if they return they do so with some knowledge of the price of their asceticism. Many critical things can be said of Rumspringa.[13] Are these teenagers really receiving an adequate picture of the outside world in such an artificial cultural experiment? Are they truly as free as advertised to make a choice to leave, especially when every aspect of their lives, including their most important relations to other persons, is encased in their solidarity with their Amish home? Is it even possible to conceive of such kinds of choices occurring authentically in these pressured, all-or-nothing moments? These are hard questions to answer, but the point I am drawing attention to is that there is *something* in place within the Amish social practices that echoes concerns about the role authenticity should play in regulating the quality of one's solidarity with a community.

Nevertheless, worries about control and indoctrination through clothing remain. In early July 2009 in Khartoum, Sudan, several women were arrested at a popular café for wearing trousers.[14] The wearing of trousers by women is interpreted as an instance of indecency against Islamic law by some radical leaders of that region. The alleged indecency consists in the way that trousers on women are taken by some in that community as an impious transgression of gender norms in a manner that subverts "nature." The international media has put their spotlight on Lubna Hussein, one of the women arrested in the café, because she has decided to take her case to trial. She was quoted as saying, "This is a case about annulling the article that addresses women's dress code, under the

DANIEL YIM

title of indecent acts. This is my battle. This article is against the constitution and even against Islamic law itself."[15]

Hussein is a thoroughly committed member of her community with whom she stands in solidarity, but she also positions herself as an important critic and reformer who is asserting her autonomy as well as assessing the authenticity of her own convictions.[16] The beautiful thing is that she and her supporters who showed up to preliminary court proceedings wearing trousers are using something as mundane as apparel to proclaim their solidarity, much like the American Olympic medalists Smith and Carlos who used items such as a scarf and gloves to express their solidarity with their oppressed community and their critique of the larger community whose silence on issues of racial and social justice needed attention.

While it is no doubt true that traditions surrounding clothing are abused as a means of control and indoctrination, they can be deployed as vehicles for reform. They are also a wonderful way that communities display their loyalty. I suppose that sensibilities about clothing are like any social practice that is connected to communal association: beautiful and ennobling when used virtuously, destructive and dehumanizing when abused.

The focus thus far has been on specifically political and religious communities of solidarity and their distinctive dress codes. The reason is that communities with a tight ideological core are easy to identify. There are, however, many communities with less formal affiliations that communicate their solidarity and critique by means of distinctive apparel in equally interesting ways.

I grew up watching documentaries of the 1960s. I was fascinated by the hippie wardrobe and crazy unkempt hair. It was only much later as an adult that I came to realize that there was method in the madness. This is hardly a place to give a history lesson on the 1960s, and I am not qualified to do so. However, one aspect that does not take a specialist to notice is the way that hippie fashion decisions were symbolic of a rejection of the buttoned up 1950s era and an engagement with something they thought was genuinely new. The purposeful androgyny of the bell-bottomed jeans, mini-skirts that hyperbolically accentuated potent and public sexuality, psychedelic prints that called to mind altered states of drug-induced awareness, and the abandonment in many cases of the bra are examples of several motifs that represent layers of social commentary by this community, ranging from simple rejection of their parents' conventions to more complex utopian visions having to do with global peace and the beginnings of a new racial and gender consciousness.

My era is a much less idealistic than the one in the 1960s. We still have utopians in the city, however. In my region, the most obvious and perhaps internally consistent ones are devout practitioners of veganism. The avoidance of animal products of any kind (not just with respect to food) is quite a challenge. The reasons that vegans give for choosing this diet and lifestyle are diverse, but they usually cluster around moral, religious, and spiritual bases. The avoidance of animal products, by necessity, has spawned a small industry of vegan ensembles, dubbed "cruelty-free clothing."

Before I was personally acquainted with any vegans, I stereotyped them as hippie-wannabes who neither dressed nor ate very well due to their extreme asceticism. Vegans, however, are quite diverse in their appearance. They can choose to wear their veganism on their sleeves quite literally through choices that visibly identify them as adherents of an eco-ethic such as veganism (though they do have to work a little at distinguishing themselves from the more general "granola crowd"). They can also take advantage of subtler, brand-based products where their allegiance to the eco-friendly ethic of veganism can take more sophisticated and even secret forms. On a segment of *The Today Show* from 2007, *Lucky* magazine featured several vegan accessories ranging from handbags to shoes and belts.[17] What makes this instance so interesting is the way fashion is used to associate with communities of the likeminded. One can now make choices to associate with veganism in the same way one might make choices to align one's consumer ethic with something like Fair Trade products. It has become less about portraying one's association for display to others and more about doing what one believes is right by one's conscience. Doing the latter need not be visible to be valuable. Perhaps there is also the delight that comes from *secret* associations that only those in the know can recognize. In the case of cruelty-free clothing, the marks of these products are recognizable only to those who know what to look for, and this creates a dual layered solidarity in terms of the shared moral values articulated through the products and the rush that comes from being part of a selective, even secretive, club.

Despite this underground expression of vegan sensibilities, the identifiable, stable ideological core of veganism has natural, limiting implications for its products: construction by means of cruelty-free raw materials. There are much looser confederations of the likeminded that are nevertheless tied together in solidarity by specific items of dress. In the 1970s, for whatever reason the Levis 501 jean became iconic for the gay community in America. This is evidenced by the 2008 Gus Van

  DANIEL YIM

Sant film *Milk*, which chronicles the political rise and eventual assassination of San Francisco activist Harvey Milk. Van Sant very intentionally and prominently featured Levis 501s in wardrobe decisions to highlight this community's historic and continuing struggle for recognition and dignity.

Fashion also played a central role in the formation and maintenance of the diverse community at Smith College in the 1920s.[18] Smith College was founded as a women's college in the late 1800s in Massachusetts. In addition to the main college activity of studying, much of their communal life was organized around fashion, including social activities such as shopping, constructing their own clothing out of textiles, styling hair according to prevailing trends, and so on. This suggests an additional layer of complexity in the way their conscientiousness about fashion was marshaled to maintain their communal ties. While they did share some style motifs, they were far looser than codes *per se*. Instead, these activities functioned as a common context, like a "living room," for many of their other important social practices that were mentioned above. In that respect, it was more the total phenomenon of being fashion-conscious than a particular style code that formed the crucible for their college experience and solidarity. One element that was popular among the young women of Smith College was termed "collegiate style." This included, among other things, tweed suits and the bob haircut (which signaled sexual energy and liberation to some). They used this presentation to project the image of the serious woman scholar who was simultaneously "feminine" by 1920s standards. They were in the unenviable position of responding to critics who thought that women's education was an oxymoron and to those who thought that the education of women would unbalance society. A century of hindsight and social progress may tempt us to view their efforts with mixed opinions, but what is noteworthy for present purposes is that they chose fashion as a vehicle for expressing both their solidarity with each other and their responses to the critical attention they received from outside their community.

In a brief essay of this nature, it simply is not possible to do full justice to the overwhelming range of clothing, style, and the way that they have been used to articulate autonomy, authenticity, and, perhaps most interestingly, communal solidarity. History is replete with examples of this occurring in every recorded human culture in every period of their respective existence. Articulations range from gravely serious to hilariously comic. The epicycles of these processes, even within just one culture, are endless. My modest goal has been to raise our appreciation of the connection between the social practices involving the adornment of our bodies and properties that contribute to a good human life. I chose my examples in the hope that they would connect widely with several different types of readers who would be led to consider further contexts where dress plays this important role in human life. It is within such contexts that the larger phenomenon of fashion for me becomes not just interesting but also a worthwhile subject of philosophical and anthropological investigation. After all, we are what we wear.

NOTES

1 Kathleen Kiley Wade and Mary E. Stafford, "Public School Uniforms: Effect on Perceptions of Gang Presence, School Climate, and Student Self-perceptions," *Education and Urban Society* 35 (2003): 399–420.
2 Wendell Anderson, "School Dress Codes and Uniform Policies," Policy Report 4, ERIC ED471528, 2002, accessed August 27, 2009.http://www.eric.ed.gov/ERICWebPortal/custom/portlets/recordDetails/detailmini.jsp?_nfpb=true&_&ERICExtSearch_SearchValue_0=ED471528&ERICExtSearch_SearchType_0=no&accno=ED471528 (accessed July 23, 2009).
3 Anabel Unity Sale, "Dress to Impress," *Community Care* 1700 (November 2007): 34.
4 Hélène Cixous, "Sonia Rykiel in Translation," translated by Deborah Jenson, in *On Fashion*, ed. Shari Benstock and Suzanne Ferris (New Brunswick: Rutgers University Press, 1994), p. 97. More information about Sonia Rykiel may be found at her website: http://www.soniarykiel.com/(accessed July 23, 2009).
5 Marilyn Friedman, "Autonomy, Social Disruption, and Women," in *Relational Autonomy: Feminist Perspectives on Autonomy, Agency and the Social Self*, eds Natalie Stoljar and Catriona Mackenzie (Oxford: Oxford University Press, 2000), pp. 35–51.
6 "Locavore" refers to a person who is committed to eating only locally sourced foods.
7 Bob Egelko, "S.F. Slaying of Dad, Sons Called Gang Related," *San Francisco Chronicle*, July 29, 2008, B3.
8 Tamara Barak Aparton, "S.F. Man ID'd as Victim of Fatal Shooting," *San Francisco Examiner*, February 23, 2009, http://www.sfexaminer.com/local/SF-man-IDd-as-victim-of-fatal-shooting-40071122.html (accessed July 23, 2009).
9 Anat Helman, "Kibbutz Dress in the 1950s: Utopian Equality, Anti Fashion, and Change," *Fashion Theory* 12 (2008): 313–340.

10 Joe Wittmer, "Homogeneity of Personality Characteristics: A Comparison between Old Order Amish and Non-Amish," *American Anthropologist*, New Series, 72: (1970): 1063–1068.

11 Vanessa O'Connell, "Fashion Bullies Attack," *Wall Street Journal*, October 25, 2007, D1.

12 National Public Radio Morning Edition Archives, "Amish Teens Tested in 'Devil's Playground'," http://www.npr.org/programs/morning/features/2002/may/amish/ (accessed July 23, 2009).

13 Steven V. Mazie, "Consenting Adults? Amish Rumspringa and the Quandary of Exit in Liberalism," *Perspectives on Politics* 3 (2005): 745–759.

14 Tristan McConnell, "Tear Gas Fired at Protesters Outside Lubna Hussein Trial," *Times Online*, August 5, 2009, http://www.timesonline.co.uk/tol/news/world/africa/article6738594.ece (accessed August 6, 2009).

15 Guardian UK World News Archives, "Sudanese Journalist Quits UN Job to Go on Trial for Wearing Trousers," July 30, 2009, http://www.guardian.co.uk/world/2009/jul/30/sudanese-journalist-trial-trousers (accessed August 2, 2009).

16 The case is still ongoing at the time of the writing of this essay, and so I cannot report on how the case turns out.

17 Today Show Fashion and Beauty Archives, "Animal-friendly Accessories for Hipsters," http://www.msnbc.msn.com/id/18269937/ (accessed July 23, 2009).

18 Kendra Van Cleave, "A Style All Her Own: Fashion, Clothing Practices, and Female Community at Smith College, 1920–1929," *Dress* 32 (2005): 56–65.

CHAPTER 8

FASHION AND SEXUAL IDENTITY, OR WHY RECOGNITION MATTERS

Why should political philosophers think about fashion? What is political about our individual style and fashion choices? I am a feminist political philosopher who is interested in exploring questions about the political and ethical significance of fashion in the context of debates about sexual citizenship, identity politics, and rights to recognition. My thoughts in this area are shaped partly by debates about the political strategy of visibility in advancing the cause of gay, lesbian, and bisexual equality and partly by my own personal experiences in the area of sexual orientation and fashion. By the end of the exploration I hope to have persuaded you that political philosophers ought to think about fashion and its implications and that fashion raises some difficult and interesting questions in political philosophy.

In a way it is odd to think about fashion in the context of political philosophy because philosophers as a group have not taken fashion at all seriously. Indeed, there is a remarkable degree of disdain in the attitude of philosophers to such trivial, superficial, and unworthy matters as clothing, footwear, and hairstyles (to name just three areas in which

Fashion – Philosophy for Everyone: Thinking with Style, First Edition.
Edited by Jessica Wolfendale and Jeanette Kennett.
© 2011 Blackwell Publishing Ltd. Published 2011 by Blackwell Publishing Ltd.

standards of fashion are thought to apply). This chapter talks about fashion in the broad sense insofar as it is concerned with how we dress and adorn ourselves. I do not reserve talk of fashion for "high fashion" or cutting edge, runway worthy fashion. But I am not so broad as to include all aspects of our lives to which fashionable standards might apply. One can talk about fashionable noses (in a world where cosmetic surgery is common) or fashionable ideas or fashionable neighborhoods. These fashionable things are beyond the scope of this essay. So it is both "low" and "high" fashion that interests me but I restrict my interests to clothing and footwear choices, make up, and hairstyles.

In an essay in the feminist philosophy journal *Hypatia* called "Dressing Down, Dressing up: The Philosophic Fear of Fashion," Karen Hanson takes on philosophers' fear of fashion. She notes that the disdain for talking about clothing is interesting, and almost certainly gendered, since philosophers have no difficulty conversing about food, music, and household furnishings.[1] At a dinnertime gathering of philosophers the conversation is as likely to be about wine or recent films as it is to be about abiding philosophical problems. While these are allowed as acceptable topics for discussion among academics, what to wear to a faculty council meeting and the reception at the president's house afterward is not.[2] Raising the topic of what this summer's dresses will be like or what one thinks of the clothes featured in a particular television show, say *Mad Men*, for example, is even worse. One who dares broach the topic will have confessed an interest in a subject that the group agrees bespeaks vanity or worse. Thomas H. Benton, in his account of trying to dress formally as a professor, accounts for the hostility towards thinking about fashion in terms of income: "Professors (in the humanities, at least) don't make much money relative to other professionals, so we press our sour grapes into the sweeter wine of smugness: 'We are too important to pay attention to such trivial, privileged matters as clothing.' 'One day you put on a tie, the next day you are driving a Hummer and voting Republican.'"[3] But it can't just be money and politics that explains our contempt for caring about clothing for the fear of fashion extends to well-paid academics and includes those whose political allegiances are beyond reproach.

Indeed, Hanson claims that the philosophical disdain for concern with clothing extends back to Plato. "The healthy state" that Socrates describes in Book II of the *Republic* has citizens in "summer for the most part unclad and unshod and in the winter clothed and shod sufficiently"; and this community remains content with simple garb, with a simple life, as they "hand on a like life to their offspring."[4] But nothing is as simple as it seems and philosophers ought to be wary of claims about what is simple and natural. Writes Hanson: "Clothing is a part of our difficult, post-Edenic lives; and dress, stationed at a boundary between self and other, marking a distinction between private and public, individual and social, is likely to be vexed by the forces of border wars. Philosophers, those who believe that the life worth living is the examined life, should find that willful ignorance of these matters ill suits them."[5] I like Hanson's focus on fashion as sitting on the fence between public and private and between the individual and the social. Fashion, as an enterprise is an activity one undertakes keeping in mind both personal style and the need to communicate with others to others.

One might think you would do better consulting feminist philosophers if you were interested in fashion and political philosophy. After all, feminists typically have a much broader lens for critical interest, seeing many things worthy of scrutiny that others have dismissed as philosophically uninteresting. Feminist philosophers got us to see the everyday lives of men and women as philosophically interesting for the role that gender socialization and enforced gender norms played in shaping women's and men's lives. The slogan "the personal is political" indicated that much of what seemed purely personal had in fact a political element and this was worthy of feminist attention. So feminists and feminist philosophers have not totally ignored fashion. However, feminist work on fashion has largely been critical of fashion as a tool of male domination. Feminists have rightly noticed how many fashion trends have the effect of making women's bodies less mobile and less physically powerful. From corsets and high heels to burkas and bound feet, fashion trends targeted at women around the world seem inextricably linked with the sexual exploitation of women by men.[6] The combination of misogynist fashion with capitalism leads to further sources of feminist outrage. Feminist political theorists examine the global sweatshops where most 'fashionable' clothes are produced. Feminist economists calculate the 'beauty tax' – the extra cost borne by women maintaining the minimal standards of beauty required to attract a partner and keep a job. Women also pay more than men for a wide range of everyday items. Sometimes this is explicit such as in the different price attached to dry cleaning a men's versus a women's shirt, and the different prices for cutting men's and women's hair, while at other times it is just the case that products likely to attract women or marketed to women cost more than similar products likely to attract men or marketed to men.[7] So it is no wonder feminist philosophers have run from the subject of fashion – hands in the air, screaming – preferring to leave it alone and not think about it too much. We feminist philosophers have had a disdain for taking fashion seriously that I want to suggest is mistaken.

In a very interesting book called *Fresh Lipstick: Redressing Feminism and Fashion* Linda Scott raises troubles for the feminist preference for women's natural appearance. The "natural" is a difficult category to pin down and the boundaries between "natural" and "socially constructed" can be hard to locate. The feminist tendency to prefer a certain style as natural can raise difficulties for women whose shapes and bodies don't so easily fit. "As long as we ignore the fact that all women also belong to other groups – different classes, races, and religions – we can turn a blind eye to the reality that some women have advantages over others and have in the past, acted alongside men of their own class to secure those privileges. By asserting that all women must dress the same way – conform to the same 'ideal' – we make a space where we can overlook their unequal access to the goods used in grooming and dress, as well as the ethnic differences that cause each group to view particular items, colors, or methods as acceptable, beautiful, or immoral."[8]

Let me give some examples of the sort of thing that is meant here. We academic feminists have a preference for a certain look. I can often spot other women headed to the same conference as me at airports, even if we haven't met. Here are some clues. For the most part we have "wash and go" hair. Elaborate hairstyles are rare. But how easy and acceptable "wash and go" hair is depends on race and on income. A very good haircut (usually combined with expensive styling products) makes our tousled hairstyles possible. The same is true for our preference for our low heeled, understated comfortable shoes that are themselves often far more expensive than trendy alternatives.

Here is another example of unnoticed privilege related to fashion, from the work of a disability theorist. In the discussion period which followed her paper "Your Wheelchair Is So Slim: A Meditation on the Social Enactment of Beauty and Disability" Samantha Walsh talked about her choice to wear high heels and fishnets which she finds makes it easier for people to see her as an adult.[9] Dressed in ordinary clothes she is often mistaken for a child but the contrast between "child" and "fishnets" is so stark that this fashion strategy is an easy way for her to get the privilege that able-bodied women take for granted.[10] Prior to hearing Walsh's paper I confess that it had not occurred to me that the extra steps disabled women must make to be seen as adult sexual beings include choices about hosiery and heels. In this case fashion works as a communicative strategy, this time against the predominant stereotypes of disability. According to Diane Richardson, there are special problems for disabled citizens in accessing the rights of sexual citizenship. She writes: "Stereotypes of disability, for example, include assumptions of asexuality; of lack of sexual potential. While historically there has been minimal discussion of the sexual politics of disability, both within disability studies and work on sexuality, in recent years attempts have been made to place sexual rights on the political agenda of disability movements ... A particular focus has been the ways in which people with disabilities have been denied the capacity for sexual feeling and rights to sexual expression."[11]

Not worrying about fashion, or claiming to, is itself a sign of privilege. Sometimes this is because one has so thoroughly tutored oneself in certain norms they become invisible. But outsiders need to learn them. The studied casual look that most academics sport can be as difficult to get just right as the most formal of suits. And even when male academics get it wrong – as for example, when they wear socks with sandals or white tube socks with dark suits – they can afford not to care for very little or nothing rides on their appearance. Within academia, women worry more than men about how to dress for our roles. Men might find this trivial but they are not so often in the position of being mistaken for administrative staff, or in the case of young women professors, graduate students. The power of role and rank in decisions about personal appearance was brought home to me recently when I became a full professor (capital "P" Professor unmodified as opposed to Assistant Professor and then Associate Professor) and decided to get several tattoos. Prior to attaining the rank of Professor I would not have said that I dressed to fit in the academic community but once I was promoted I found myself reconsidering my options in the realm of personal presentation. The thought "What can they do? I'm a Professor" has come up often enough that I can see that my former view, that I was not trying to fit in, was based on self-deception.

The Sexual Citizen, Rights to Recognition, and Visibility as a Strategy

Having established that fashion matters and that philosophers ought to care, I want to think about fashion in the context of sexual citizenship, rights of recognition, and the strategy of visibility. Let's start with the concept of the sexual citizen. Moral and political philosophy in the liberal tradition has typically described citizens in the language of abstract and idealized personhood. On this account, the citizen is perfectly rational and autonomous and finds his/her home in the public realm. Feminists have criticized this concept of the disembodied citizen as either smuggling in norms of masculinity (and so not really abstract at all) or as impossibly unrealistic as the basis on which to build moral and political theory. Queer theorists have likewise criticized the liberal citizen as attached to the norms of heterosexuality and as entrenching the public/private divide. Insofar as gay, lesbian, and bisexual rights claims get voice in the liberal account it is in the public realm – in the workplace, the legislature, the courtroom – and all mention of sexuality itself is left at home in the private. But this ignores public expressions of queer sexuality and allows in gay, lesbian, and bisexual moral and political agency only when sexuality is abstracted away. In contrast to the abstract citizen of liberal political philosophy, the alternative account of the citizen, the sexual citizen moves in the public realm as a sexual being. According to *GLBTQ Encyclopedia of Culture*, the "sexual citizen" bridges the private and public, and stresses the cultural and political sides of sexual expression. Sexual privacy cannot exist without open sexual cultures. Homosexuality might be consummated in the bedroom, but first partners must be found in the public space of "streets, bars, and media such as newspapers and the internet."[12] Cultural theorist Jeffrey Weeks puts the point this way: "The 'sexual citizen' is a recent phenomenon. Making private claims to space, self-determination and pleasure, and public claims to rights, justice and recognition." Weeks writes that the sexual citizen is a hybrid being, who tells us a great deal about political and cultural transformation and new possibilities of the self and identity.[13]

Political theorists writing about citizenship have identified two aspects of citizenship. The first is about rights, such as equal access to institutions and equal status before the law. The second is about recognition: the establishment of a political relationship and being recognized as a fellow citizen. Shane Phelan argues that barriers to citizenship for gays and lesbians, and other sexual minorities, are often found in this second category:

> In contrast with most women and racial minorities, sexual minorities have a varying ability to be hidden, to leave their difference "suppressed or left uncertain." And this is how many, if not most, heterosexuals would like

them to remain. Many who express support for the legal rights of sexual minorities nonetheless express desire that "those people" keep their difference invisible.[14]

Phelan writes that within a heterosexual world, heterosexuality is presumed: just as white is a default category among whites, seemingly "unraced" or neutral, heterosexuality is a position that is so unremarkable among heterosexuals that it becomes invisible as a structure.[15] Gays, lesbians, and bisexuals are thus accused of "flaunting" when we make our sexuality obvious but heterosexuality can be enacted and go unremarked. In Phelan's words, "Thus many heterosexuals express a tolerance for homosexuals, but object to 'flaunting it,' arguing that they not make a public display of their own sexuality. In fact, however, every marriage ceremony, every coffee break discussion, every induction exam is a site for heterosexual display." Thus the political strategy of visibility had a certain necessity to it. According to Phelan, a group that is consistently present only as the opposite or outside the nation, that has no part in the national imaginary except as threat, cannot participate in citizenship, no matter what rights its members have come to enjoy.[16]

As a strategy visibility is connected to the quest for rights of recognition. One of the main rights claimed on behalf of the sexual citizen is the right of recognition. Queer theorists have argued that gay men, lesbians, and bisexuals do not merely want the same rights as the sexual majority. Rather a large part of what the queer community wants is to be recognized as having legitimate identity. That is, queer activists want to be recognized as queer citizens. Lisa Walker writes: "Privileging visibility has become a tactic of late twentieth-century identity politics, in which participants often symbolize their demands for social justice by celebrating visible signifiers of difference that have historically targeted them for discrimination."[17]

Some people object at this point that sexuality and sexual orientation are private matters. But only from the perspective of the privileged sexual orientation is sexuality private. We need to find ways to communicate our sexual orientation to others for a wide range of purposes, not the least of which is the burden of continual explanation. Sexuality is also a legal matter. Even within the liberal state there are a wide range of laws regulating sexuality. These laws – even when we agree with them – still shape the range of permissible sexual acts and lifestyles. Sexuality is also a cultural matter. Recognition as a sexual citizen, being seen as a group member, being able to speak as a member of a group, is often not something an individual can will to do. Recognition will depend on issues of power, appearance, and context.

Let me give an example, familiar to most people with an alternative gender or sexual identity. It is relatively easy can be seen and identified as a queer femme in Toronto or San Francisco while in smaller towns and cities, such an option doesn't exist. A queer femme takes on a gender identity which is in some respects traditionally or stereotypically feminine while at the same time having a queer sexual identity. Queer femininity is usually more accentuated and intentional than a straight female gender identity or gender presentation and often challenges standards of femininity through exaggeration, parody, or transgression of gender norms. But to dress in a feminine fashion is, in some locations, outside urban areas, to invite being misread as straight. To understand this point we need to return to the point that fashion occurs at the boundary of the personal and the political, at the edge between private and public. Fashion achievements require the right community. It can never be an individual enterprise. Here are some more examples to help make this point. You can't wear a trucker cap ironically in a community in which trucker caps are worn seriously. Successful irony requires the right set of background conditions. Fishnets and combat boots only work as a fashion statement when you're somewhere people won't just assume you cannot afford heels or that you have made a mistake. While the identity "boi" is easily available in urban settings, the best you might manage in other environments is baby butch. (A boi is a transgendered/androgynous/masculine person who is biologically female and presents themselves in a young, boyish way, according to the urban dictionary.) This is also generation specific. There were no bois when I came out in the 1980s. Trans and other gender queer identities are now more easy to access and live. Could you have been a boi in the 1980s? In the absence of a community which recognizes and affirms your identity, probably not. Likewise, you can stuff your pockets with colored hankies all you want but in the absence of a leather community with shared understanding of what various colors and their placement mean regarding your sexual preferences, you aren't flagging. You're just wearing a hanky in your pocket. (One can also make the point that you couldn't create your own hanky code with your own meanings attached to the various colors. Such efforts would be meaningless. Call this Wittingstein's "private hanky" argument.) All of these examples are just to make the point that fashion is essentially communicative and what is possible as identity will depend in part on what identity categories exist in the community in which you find yourself.

The lesson here is that being out and being visible is easier for some than for others. In her book *Looking Like What You Are: Sexual Style, Race, and Lesbian Identity*, Lisa Walker tackles this problem from the perspective of lesbian identity and the problem of recognition for women who are lesbians but who aren't seen as such. In Walker's chapter, "How to Recognize a Lesbian," she argues that there are both benefits and costs to strategies of visibility. Walker focuses on the identity issues facing lesbians who identify as femme. There are many statements of femme identity in various new collections of essays about femme – see for example, *Visible: A Femmethology* Volumes 1 and 2, and *Brazen Femme, A Femme's Guide to the Universe*[18] – but I find the most poignant expression of the costs of being femme in an essay by the butch author Ivan Coyote. In a piece entitled "Hats Off to Beautiful Femmes" Ivan Coyote writes:

> I know that sometimes you feel like nobody truly sees you. I want you to know that I see you. I see you on the street, on the bus, in the gym, in the park. I don't know why I can tell that you are not straight, but I can. Maybe it is the way you look at me. Please don't stop looking at me the way you do … I would never say that the world is harder on me than it is you. Sometimes you are invisible. I have no idea what this must feel like, to pass right by your people and not be recognized. To not be seen … I want to thank you for coming out of the closet. Again and again, over and over, for the rest of your life. At school, at work, at your kid's daycare, at your brother's wedding, at the doctor's office. Thank you for sideswiping their stereotypes.[19]

While Walker's work examines visibility from the perspective of the femme lesbian, there are other issues tied to recognition and visibility. Recognition is an important theme in queer culture and queer politics. Note that recognition has two aspects. First, there is recognition by the members of one's own group. This can matter even more in contexts in which public recognition is too dangerous and so systems of secret signals develop, such as wearing a single earring in a particular ear. It still matters though even in contexts in which secrecy is not important and even if you think it does not matter. Consider that there is a definite loss when that sense of recognition disappears. I think of my own experiences travelling and what it was like to find that in some countries I could not recognize lesbians as lesbians. In certain places in the world it seemed to me that no one was queer. In still other places, my mistakes went the other way. It seemed to me that most of the women looked queer. This mattered to me more than I thought it ought to. Second, there is

SAMANTHA BRENNAN

recognition by a larger community and this can be more difficult to accomplish as it requires education on the part of a larger group. Coyote and Walker are talking about both kinds of recognition in their discussions of femme invisibility. In this chapter I am mostly talking about recognition as a single phenomenon though the reality is much more complex.

One way we recognize one another is by dressing like a dyke. But what do lesbians wear? Debate about lesbian fashion aesthetics opened up recently in Canada in the light of Canada's first lesbian clothing store, Boutique Mad-ame. The store opened in Montreal in 2006 and closed a couple of years later. On the store website the store's owner posed the question, "What is a lesbian aesthetic?"[20] She notes that obviously lesbians were dressing themselves before the store opened and there certainly isn't a dyke uniform. Criteria for inclusion in the store were a disjunct of various political criteria. All the store's items were either organic, fair trade, made or designed in Quebec, or designed by a lesbian. The store also offered tailoring and aimed to take into account a wide range of sizes and varying gender expressions. Owner Amy Skinner was proud that her store also offered a queer friendly shopping environment. "There are places where it is not comfortable to shop with your girlfriend," she said. "If you're looking at men's clothes, you often get quips from sales staff that the clothes you're looking at are for men and you can't try on men's clothes in the men's changing rooms. Most of the lesbians I've met say stores don't address their particular interests."

The mainstream media has started to pay attention too to lesbian fashion. *Salon* ran a piece entitled "Rachel Maddow, reluctant sex symbol" and The *New York Times* Spring 2009 Women's Fashion Issue also talked about Maddow in their piece "Butch Fatale: Lesbian Glamour Steps Out Of The Closet." An article called "The Subtle Power of Lesbian Style," in the *New York Times* Style Issue drew attention to increasing numbers of queer women working in the fashion industry. "There are a lot of gay women working in fashion, obviously, and they approach it as gay women, and that fashion is then consumed by a much larger culture," Ms. Chaiken said. "What makes their work lesbian fashion? It is probably that they are celebrating that play with gender, that provocative style that pulls from rock 'n' roll, boy icons of the past, the street and the high-end couture type glamour, but that starts with a lesbian sensibility." We can add to this the recent increase in the visibility of lesbian stars on mainstream television, from kd lang to Maddow, to the women of the *L Word*.

Within the queer community, the debate continues over lesbian fashion. A recent issue of Canada's leftie alternative magazine *this magazine* featured an article entitled "The Lesbian Fashion Crisis," by Cate Simpson. She writes:

> Contrary to popular belief, there is really no lesbian fashion aesthetic. There's a "look," but it is hard to quantify and even harder to emulate if you're a newcomer to the scene. It is one of those you-know-it-when-you-see-it things. And it only applies to the shorthaired stereotype-adhering among us; if you're high-femme, you're on your own. Queer women who come out in their 20s instead of in their teens seem to be hit hardest by the lesbian fashion crisis. I have more than one bisexual friend who – accustomed to dressing up to get the attention of men on a Friday night – is entirely at a loss when it comes to dressing for other women.

Continues Simpson:

> Part of the problem is that it is tough just to find clothes that fit you when you're boyish looking but shaped like a girl. Men's clothes are tentlike on us, but women's clothes are invariably too, well, woman-y. And those perfect-fitting men's-suits-cut-for-women Shane wears on *The L Word*? Those don't really exist. All of this has me wondering about the stickers that are available all through Pride Week with every conceivable sexual orientation written on them. It is as if, having shed our clothes and our coded messages about who we might sleep with, we are finally free to wear our identities on our sleeves.[21]

The worry is that insofar as a lesbian aesthetic exists it seems to necessarily exclude those who do not know what it is or how to go about enacting it. In her paper "Navigating Embodied Lesbian Cultural Space: Toward a lesbian habitus, space and culture," Alison Rooke explores themes of exclusion and inclusion in the lives of working-class lesbian and bisexual women (both transsexual and nontranssexual). Writes Rooke:

> It is worth noting that the aestheticization of lesbian and gay identities and bodies into "lifestyle" ... had become more apparent in the past 20 years. The lesbian body politic has significantly changed since the 1980s and 1990s. The lesbian feminist critique of "patriarchy" was born out through embodied practices. The lesbian feminist body was unruly, questioning the discourses of appropriate femininity by sprouting hair, changing shape, refusing constraining clothes, and so on ... Lesbian feminist culture offered the opportunity to experiment and explore dominant conceptions of gender;

it offered a space to rethink heteronormativity and for some the possibility to live, at least temporarily in space and time, outside of its bounds.[22]

But Rooke's working-class subjects were unable to fit in or to be recognized. "They fell short of a recognizable lesbian habitus in more embodied ways. They were not androgynous, gym toned, or tanned or were not displaying the appropriate haircuts. It was not merely that they did not wear the right labels. It was also the case that they did not possess the requisite cultural capital to know which brands should be worn even if they could afford them and how to wear them."[23]

While the politics of recognition seems to call for visibility as a strategy, there are dangers on relying too heavily on visibility. Writes Walker:

> While privileging visibility can be politically and rhetorically effective, it is not without its problems. Within the constraints of a particular identity that invests certain signifiers with political value, figures that do not present these signifiers are often neglected. Because subjects who can pass exceed the categories of visibility that establish identity, they tend to be understood as peripheral to the process of marginalisation … The paradigm of visibility is totalizing when a signifier of difference becomes synonymous with the identity it signifies. In this situation, members of a given population who do not bear that signifier of difference, or who bear visible signs of another identity are rendered invisible and are marginalized within an already marginalized community.[24]

Susie Bright is quoted at the beginning of Walker's chapter on looking like a lesbian: "Of course, there's a strict gay dress code no matter where you cruise. At the height of my college cruising, I was attending Take Back the Night meetings dressed in Mr. Greenjeans overalls, Birkenstocks, and a bowl hair-cut that made me look like I'd just been released from a bad foster home. There is nothing more pitiful to look at than a closeted femme."

I would like to close this chapter with a piece of personal narrative, to tell a little bit about my own story around identity and appearance. I came out as a lesbian during university, in the 1980s. Making my own sexual identity known to the world was simple. I cut my hair, started wearing what 20- year-old lesbians in the 1980s were wearing – jeans, t-shirts, Converse sneakers, significant belts, and a single earring. My favorite earring was itself also a signifier of orientation. It was in the shape of a labrys, the double-sided ax associated with Amazon warriors. I was instantly recognizable and that mattered a lot to me. It mattered for the purpose of not getting hit on by men and for the purpose of being seen by the women who I wanted to notice me. Fashion mattered. Friends, family, and colleagues reading this know I recanted on the "excluding men" part of my sexual orientation many years ago and have identified as a bisexual for more than 20 years. But now in my mid-40s it is much harder to maintain any level of visibility. The challenges relate to two important aspects of my life: having a straight male partner and kids, and aging. Often when making the point really matters, I simply label myself to avoid confusion. I have a t-shirt that reads "bi" and I wore that when giving talks based on some of the material in this paper. I sometimes wear it to class to end speculation among students. I also had a pin that read, "I'm bisexual and I'm still not attracted to you" but I'm also a nice person and that pin seemed too mean spirited. I hate to hurt feelings. It is important to note that I do not describe myself as being in a heterosexual marriage. I would like our language here to change. Orientations apply to people and not relationships. Thus a same sex marriage need not be a gay marriage. It could well be a marriage of two bisexuals. The correct contrast to same sex marriage is opposite sex marriage. And so if what you mean by a heterosexual marriage is a marriage of two heterosexuals, then mine isn't such a marriage. Aging poses a different sort of challenge for recognition. On the one hand, many of my midlife women friends match various lesbian stereotypes. We tend to have short hair, wear comfortable shoes, often don't wear make up, and some of the time seem to enjoy having escaped the male gaze. But it is also the case that women in midlife are often viewed as asexual so the categories of gender and sexual orientation fail to apply in any interesting way. I continue to struggle with visibility and the burden of explanation. I do not expect these issues to go away anytime soon.

This chapter has sprawled over a lot of different topics and themes. All I hope to have established is that insofar as fashion sits at the boundary between public and private, it ought to be of significance for moral and political philosophers. In particular, I hope to have shown that fashion has a key role to play in the political strategy of queer visibility. Finally, I hope also to have shown that are some difficulties with privileging the strategy of visibility.

NOTES

1 Karen Hanson, "Dressing Down Dressing Up – The Philosophic Fear of Fashion," *Hypatia, Special Issue: Feminism and Aesthetics* 5 (1990): 107–121.

2 There are of course some exceptions. See "Dressing Like a Professor," on *Worn Through*, a fashion professor's blog, http://www.wornthrough.com/2009/01/16/on-teaching-fashion-looking-like-a-professor/ (accessed December 7, 2010).

3 Thomas H. Benton, "The Year of Dressing Formally: An Academic in America," *The Chronicle of Higher Education*, 54 (2008), in which a college English professor details his decision to build a wardrobe that is suitable to an academic with tenure.

4 Plato, *The Republic* (Cambridge: Cambridge University Press, 1963), pp. 618–619.

5 Hanson, Karen. 1990. "Dressing down Dressing up – The Philosophic Fear of Fashion," *Hypatia* 5 (1990): pp. 107 121, p. 119.

6 See, for example, Naomi Wolf, *The Beauty Myth: How Images of Beauty Are Used against Women* (New York: Anchor, 1992).

7 For the most recent report on this topic see the January 2010 issue of *Consumer Reports* magazine according to which women pay more for a variety of drugstore items as well. Products directed at women, according to the article, might cost up to 50% more than similar products for men even when the ingredient list is the same.

8 Linda Scott, *Fresh Lipstick: Redressing Feminism and Fashion*, (Basingstoke, UK: Palgrave Macmillan, 2004), p. 13.

9 Samantha Walsh, "Your Wheelchair Is So Slim: A Meditation on the Social Enactment of Beauty and Disability." Presented at the feminist philosophy graduate student conference Diotima, Fall 2009, The University of Western Ontario.

10 The sexual rights of the disabled are discussed in Diane Richardson, "Constructing Sexual Citizenship: Theorizing Sexual Rights," *Critical Social Policy* 20 (2000): 105–135.

11 Richardson, "Sexual Citizenship," p. 105.

12 GLBTQ Encyclopedia of Culture, http://www.glbtq.com/(accessed February 12, 2011).

13 Jeffrey Weeks, "The Sexual Citizen," *Theory Culture Society* 15 (1998): 35–52.

14 Shane Phelan, *Sexual Strangers: Gays, Lesbians, and Dilemmas of Citizenship* (Philadelphia: Temple University Press, 2001), p. 15.

15 Phelan, *Sexual Strangers*, p. 35.

16 Phelan, *Sexual Strangers*, p. 7.

17 Lisa Walker, *Looking Like What You Are: Sexual Style, Race, and Lesbian Identity* (New York: NYU Press, 2001), p. 868.

18 Burke, Jennifer Clare. *Visible: A Femmethology* (Homofactus Press, 2009); Ulrika Dahl and Volcano Del LaGrace, *Femmes of Power: Exploding Queer Femininities* (Serpent's Tail Press, 2009).

19 "Hats Off to Beautiful Femmes: Thank You for Looking at Me The Way You Do," Ivan E Coyote, National xtra / Thursday, July 30, 2009

(accessed August 1, 2009). http://www.xtra.ca/public/National/Hats_off_to_beautiful_femmes-7215.aspx (accessed August 1, 2009).

20 http://askthegeek.org/madame/ (accessed December 7, 2010).

21 Simpson, Cate. "Queerly Canadian #13: The Lesbian Fashion Crisis," May 28, 2009, *This* magazine, available at http://this.org/blog/2009/05/28/queerly-canadian-lesbian-fashion/ (accessed April 20, 2011).

22 Rooke, Alison. 2007. "Navigating Embodied Lesbian Cultural Space: Toward a Lesbian Habitus," *Space and Culture* 10 (2007): 231–252, pp. 246–247.

23 Rooke, "Navigating Lesbian Space," p. 247.

24 Walker, *Looking*, p. 868.

CHAPTER 9

SLAVES TO FASHION?

Sitting calmly on his deathbed, Socrates teasingly reminds his friends that he, indeed any philosopher, is quite ready for the imminent liberation of his soul, since he has been practicing for it all his life. And his attitude to clothes and sex apparently has something to do with it.

"Do you think it befits a philosophical man to be keen about the so-called pleasures of ... sex?"
"Not at all."
"And what about the other services to the body? For instance, the possession of smart clothes and shoes, and the other bodily adornments? – do you think he values them highly, or does he disdain them...?"
"I think the genuine philosopher disdains them." [...]
"One who cares nothing for the pleasures of the body comes pretty close to being dead."
"Yes, what you say is quite true" [...]
"Truly then, Simmias, those who practice philosophy aright are cultivating dying, and for them least of all men does being dead hold any terror."[1]

The philosopher is no slave to sex, smart clothes, shoes, and adornment. He is interested in the changeless and the enduring. He is the seer, not

Fashion – Philosophy for Everyone: Thinking with Style, First Edition.
Edited by Jessica Wolfendale and Jeanette Kennett.
© 2011 Blackwell Publishing Ltd. Published 2011 by Blackwell Publishing Ltd.

the seen. He practices the separation of the soul and body, and in so doing, he practices dying. At Socrates's words, the gloom lifts, and the friends burst out laughing, at this confirmation of the stereotype of philosopher as someone half-dead already.

Whatever we should make of philosophy in light of all this, it seems obvious what the philosopher should make of fashion. Being no slave to clothes, sex, or the ephemeral, the philosopher is bound to be no slave to fashion. An informal glance around the average philosophy conference suggests that at any rate the sartorial aspect of the Socratic principle retains, still, some appeal.[2]

The principle has been thought, by some, to apply beyond the high-minded halls of philosophy. Mary Wollstonecraft denounced the "air of fashion" as a "badge of slavery," wherever it is worn.[3] Rousseau said that *no* man should concern himself with his appearance, with how he looks in the eyes of others. "What will people think?," he says, is the "grave of a man's virtue." *No* man should concern himself with appearance – and, crucially, no *man*. This is about virtue for man. And the rest of us? Rousseau famously proposes a double standard. "What will people think?" is the grave of a man's virtue, but it is "the throne of a woman's."[4] Ever a perceptive analyst of gender, Rousseau observes how women love adornment, smart clothes, and shoes:

> Almost as soon as they are born little girls love dressing up. Not content to be pretty, they must be admired. You can see by their little airs that this concern preoccupies them already, and even when they can barely understand you, you can control them by telling them what people will think of them. If you are foolish enough to try this way with little boys, it will not have the same effect. Give them their freedom and their sports, and they care very little what people think of them.[5]

The girl's obsessive concern for adornment, for appearance, betrays her as an unlikely candidate for Socrates' vision of the ideal philosopher, or Rousseau's vision of the ideal man. Never mind. She is practicing for something else. Watch, says Rousseau: watch the little girl, playing with her doll.

> The doll is the girl's special plaything; this very obviously shows her instinctive taste for her life's purpose. The physical aspect of the art of pleasing is found in one's dress, and this physical side of the art is the only one that the child can cultivate. Watch a little girl spend a day with her doll, continually changing its clothes, dressing and undressing it, trying new

LAUREN ASHWELL AND RAE LANGTON

combinations of trimmings either well or poorly matched. Her fingers are clumsy, her taste is crude, but already a tendency is shown in this endless occupation. Time passes without her knowing it, hours go by, even meals are forgotten. She is more eager for adornment than for food.[6]

She is not a philosopher, practicing to become dead. She is not a boy, practicing to become a man. She is a girl, practicing to become a woman. And what does that mean? "So far she herself is nothing, she is engrossed in her doll and all her coquetry is devoted to it. This will not always be so; in due time she will be her own doll."[7]

She is a girl, practicing to become a woman – and this means practicing to become her own doll. The path for the philosopher aspiring to liberation, and for the boy aspiring to manhood, is to attend to bodily adornment less and less. The path for the girl aspiring to womanhood is to attend to bodily adornment more and more. Bring on Barbie. Dress Barbie. *Become* Barbie.

While Rousseau was wrong about a lot, he was right about something. The norms about adornment, smart clothes, and shoes, remain as gendered as they ever were. Yes, men care about appearance too, men care about fashion too. But, typically, women care more; and for women the penalties for not caring are greater. Does that matter? If fashion is a "badge of slavery," as Wollstonecraft said, then the answer is yes. Caring too much about smart clothes and shoes may, as Socrates said, mean bondage to the body. It may, as Rousseau said, mean conforming to gendered norms.

There is an alternative diagnosis. One might think it's not fashion that keeps women down, but the wrong attitudes to fashion. What, after all, is so bad about paying attention to the body? The Socratic idealizing of independence from body, which finds its teasing apotheosis in the idealizing of *death*, is hardly an ideal to be recommended. Nor do the gendered aspects of fashion entirely damn it. Yes, fashion reinforces gender markings, fashion looms larger in women's lives than in men's; but perhaps the trouble is not fashion, but the *denigration* of fashion. What's bad is that women are pushed into norms, which are then dismissed for being women's norms.

Carolyn Beckingham defends women's pursuit of fashion and beauty in just these terms:

What we have is not a society where beauty is too highly valued, but one where it isn't valued enough, and that this is the source of much of the oppression which its pursuit is supposed to cause. I submit that what breaks women's spirit is not so much pursuing beauty as doing so while pretending that the object of the exercise isn't worth having.[8]

Her proposal is a refreshing, if controversial, response to a familiar bind, which we still face whenever we confront gendered norms. In Simone de Beauvoir's famous electrical analogy, the "male" gets to stand for both the positive and the neutral.[9] The norms for men have counted as the norms to which human beings, as such, should aspire: norms of, say, rationality, autonomy – and, perhaps, blindness to the trivialities of fashion. Women are the marked case, the negative, and their norms are different: norms of, say, intuitiveness, caring – and, perhaps, sensitivity to the trivialities of fashion. With gendered norms that fit Beauvoir's pattern, women face a choice, a familiar trade-off: be a first-rate woman and a second-rate person; or a second-rate woman and a first-rate person.

The solution? Here as elsewhere, there are competing strategies: accept the value of the male, "neutral" norms, and extend them to women; or affirm the value of the devalued "women's" norms, and extend them to men. A celebration of the feminine *merely because* it is feminine is not necessarily liberating – not if the norms marked as feminine are forced on women, or are not good for women. But neither should we reject them out of hand just because they are feminine. What feminism has done for women's moral perspectives (affirm the ethic of care!), and for women's art (affirm the beauty of quilts!), so, perhaps, feminism could do for women's interests in fashion.

So, is fashion a badge of slavery, or not? We are not going to resolve this question, but our focus will be on the dark side: the potential for slavery. We'll take a look at some different ways that fashion might enslave. We'll consider how slavery to fashion can have aspects that are physical, moral, and also epistemological. And in doing so, we are going to explore the idea that fashion is objectifying.

Objectification

A person is objectified when they are treated, in some morally salient respect, as if they were a mere object. More needs to be said about this, and shortly will be said. But let's begin by noting that the idea of objectification has had a long history in moral philosophy, and that feminism has breathed new life into it. Aristotle described the literal

LAUREN ASHWELL AND RAE LANGTON

slaves of his own time as living "tools," though without observing there might be something morally amiss with such treatment. Immanuel Kant, by contrast, built his entire moral philosophy on the wrongness of treating human beings as tools. While it is perfectly acceptable to treat inanimate things as if they are tools or instruments, people are different. For Kant, the fundamental principle of morality is that we must treat humanity never as a mere means, but always as an "end." Objectification is a moral problem. A person is to be treated always as someone of value in her own right, a being capable of choosing her own ends. She is not to be treated merely as an instrument, a tool for serving the purposes of others. People have agency, feelings, rights. Things don't. If you treat people as if they were things, then you are treating them inappropriately – as if they did not have agency, feelings or rights that they in fact do. This is a moral failure, because you are treating them as if they didn't have the value that they do, the value that sets people apart from mere things.

Pioneer feminists took up the idea of objectification with renewed vigor, and brought new applications that had remained unnoticed. While objectification occurs in many contexts, and many social relationships, it presents a special problem for women; indeed, it constitutes a central aspect of women's oppression. Rousseau, of course, had put his finger on the issue. A girl trains herself up to become a doll: a thing, an artifact, something that happens to look vaguely human, but still an object, whose movements are determined by the plans of others, whose value is determined by how it looks, and what it can be used for. Dolls are ornamental, pretty things, but things nonetheless. Mary Wollstonecraft agreed with Rousseau's description, though not his prescription: yes, she said, a girl is indeed trained up to become a doll. But what he describes is women's oppression, not women's ideal destiny. Yes, women are treated as "alluring objects," as slaves, as playthings; but this is a fact to be fought, not celebrated.[10] Beauvoir took up the theme again, in *The Second Sex*, "What peculiarly signalizes the situation of woman is that she – a free and autonomous being like all human creatures – nevertheless finds herself living in a world where men ... propose to stabilize her as an object."[11]

The central idea here is that of an *autonomous* being whose autonomy is, somehow, pushed out of the picture. You treat someone as a thing when you deny their autonomy, their capacity for choice. Another important idea is that of instrumentality: you treat someone as a thing when you treat them as a tool, as a mere means to your ends. These two ideas of autonomy-denial and instrumentality are present in Kant, and they occupy a core place in Martha Nussbaum's classic study of objectification.[12]

Nussbaum takes objectification to be a 'cluster concept', resistant to definition in terms of necessary and sufficient conditions. She pulls together the following cluster, seven ways to "treat someone as a thing":

1 *Instrumentality:* one treats it as a tool of one's own purposes.
2 *Denial of autonomy:* one treats it as lacking in autonomy and self-determination.
3 *Inertness:* one treats it as lacking in agency and activity.
4 *Fungibility:* one treats it as interchangeable (a) with other things of the same type, and/or (b) with things of other types.
5 *Violability:* one treats it as lacking in boundary-integrity, as something that it is permissible to break up, smash, break into.
6 *Ownership:* one treats it as something that is owned by another, can be bought or sold, etc.
7 *Denial of subjectivity:* one treats it as something whose experience and feelings (if any) need not be taken into account.[13]

Nussbaum's thought is that we have here a cluster of different ideas, orbiting around that central core, constituted by the concepts of autonomy-denial and instrumentality. Note that one might wish to add still more features to Nussbaum's seven: for example, reduction to mere appearance, and reduction to mere body.[14]

As Nussbaum herself argues, slaves, literal slaves, provide a paradigm case of objectification: as the human tools Aristotle described, they are treated as instruments; their autonomy is thwarted; they are treated as items that can be possessed, and bought and sold; they treated as fungible, treated as substitutable for something else that can do the job equally well; their subjective thoughts and feelings do not count; and they are often treated as mere bodies, useful machines.

To what extent might these ideas about objectification apply to fashion? No one would wish to trivialize the evils of institutional slavery; no one supposes that people are "slaves to fashion" in just same way that Aristotle's slaves were slaves to Aristotle. Slaves, for one thing, are enslaved to someone else, some particular individual, against a backdrop of institutions that make the slave into property. But this pattern needn't hold for all objectification. Although historical slavery may provide a paradigm case, people may also be treated as objects by diffuse social systems; and there can also be self-objectification, of the sort Rousseau described. Both of these may be in play, when it comes to the darker side of fashion.

LAUREN ASHWELL AND RAE LANGTON